HEARTS

The Diary of an Incredible Season

Mike Smith

BLACK & WHITE PUBLISHING

First published 2006
by Black & White Publishing Ltd
99 Giles Street, Edinburgh, EH6 6BZ

ISBN 13   9 781845 02 873
ISBN 10   1 84502 087 1

A CIP catalogue record for this book is available from the British Library.

Typeset by Refinecatch Limited, Bungay, Suffolk

Printed and bound by
Creative Print and Design Group Ltd

ACKNOWLEDGEMENTS

At the risk of sounding like one of those God-awful speeches you hear on the television (or at family weddings), I would still like to thank a few people who helped me with this book (so if you don't like it I can pass the buck!).

My thanks go to everyone at Black & White Publishing, particularly to Alison McBride and Patricia Marshall who both helped me enormously with the production of the book and to Gillian Mackay for the publicity; to two of the finest Hearts players ever to have graced Tynecastle – Steven Pressley and Craig Gordon – for giving me their valuable time to be interviewed; to Clare Cowan at Hearts who helped arrange my interviews with the two players; and to SNS Group who supplied the photographs for this book.

Appreciation is also due to Dave Henderson and the good people at jambos.net for their kind words of encouragement. It's still the best Hearts fans' website for the more discerning Hearts supporter.

Thanks also to Gordon Robertson, who has decided to get married in the middle of next season, Rob Muir, who has decided to head off for a life in Norway in the middle of next season, and Gary Copland, who, being a Hibee, probably won't buy this book anyway, for their encouragement and pints of foaming ale at times of need. And to my wife Pat, known to readers of jambos.net as the infamous Mrs Smith, for her support and patience during these last few months when I've been locked in the spare room with a laptop (it's not what you think, dear!).

And finally to Vladimir Romanov, who, it should be remembered, saved Heart of Midlothian Football Club from almost certain extinction – I have no doubt that selling Tynecastle and moving to Murrayfield would have meant a slow, painful death for this great Edinburgh and Scottish football institution.

Mike Smith
May 2006

www.freewebs.com/mikegsmith/

www.jambos.net

CONTENTS

This book is dedicated to the memory of my late father, who gave me the encouragement to write in the first place, and to my little diamond of a grandson, one-year-old Jack Peacock, who has brought such joy and renewed pride into my life.

JULY

June 2005. I lay on the sunlounger in my back garden with the sun beating down on my weed-strewn lawn, The Undertones on the MP3 player and a can of John Smith's bitter at my feet.

'So,' I said to the infamous Mrs Smith as she struggled with the lawn mower, 'do you fancy a long weekend in Dublin?'

'When?' she snapped in her own inimitable style.

'How about the second weekend in July? I'll see if I can get a couple of days off work and we can spend a few nights in the Emerald Isle.'

She gave me that all-too familiar wry look but changed her mood with all the speed of a Paul Hartley free kick as she considered her reply. 'All right,' she sniped, 'even *I* know there's no football at that time of year so I know you won't disappear like you normally do.'

We flew out from Edinburgh airport on the morning of Saturday 9 July. Her suspicions were aroused when she spotted more than one passenger on the Ryanair flight wearing a Hearts top. By the time we reached Dublin city centre, less than ninety minutes later the game was up.

'There's a bloody Hearts game on, isn't there?'

Of course there was. And so began a most remarkable season, that of 2005/06, which had its beginnings on Hearts pre-season tour of the Republic of Ireland and a friendly against old European adversaries St Patrick's Athletic. Barely a fortnight earlier, Hearts supporters were in turmoil. The summer of 2005 had seen little respite from the drama that had engulfed Hearts for the last twelve months.

The summer of 2004 had seen a host of players leave the club and just two – Ramon Pereira and Jamie McAllister – arrive. Head Coach Craig Levein had yet again seen his budget for players slashed and one wondered how many more miracles the big Fifer could produce. With Hearts' debt approaching £19m, season 2004/05 was being signalled by Chief Executive Chris Robinson as the club's last at its spiritual home – Tynecastle Stadium. Plans were afoot to sell Tynecastle to property developers and to move Hearts to Murrayfield Stadium – home of Scottish Rugby and an arena with a 67,500 capacity that would have more than 50,000 empty seats for most home games. The fans were in uproar. Robinson was never going to win any popularity awards in Gorgie but he turned into something of a hate figure with this latest half-baked idea. Fans held protest marches, the Save Our Hearts campaign worked tirelessly to fight the sale of Tynecastle and fans were genuinely concerned that a famous football institution was about to be served its last rites.

Although the decision to sell the famous old stadium was taken by the board of directors, many fans saw

Robinson as the villain of the piece. Only a year earlier, the Chief Executive had proposed Hearts selling Tynecastle and moving to Straiton, on the outskirts of Edinburgh to share a 30,000 capacity stadium with a team from Leith. Whilst the location would have seen Heart of Midlothian actually playing in Midlothian, this grand idea was never going to see the light of day with far too many obstacles such as planning permission and the possibility of old mine shafts on the land identified for the stadium to be overcome.

When Hibernian announced they had no intention of leaving the cultural metropolis that is Leith, the Straiton project was dead in the water. With the huge debt crippling the club, desperation set in. Chris Robinson and his board of directors then signed a tentative agreement with a housing organisation to sell Tynecastle for £24 million. With Tynecastle Park being reduced to rubble, Hearts would move to Murrayfield – with no visible sign of a plan to build a custom-built stadium or any alternative scheme that would rescue the club from certain oblivion. Many fans had stopped going to Hearts games as a result of the board's policies in any case – how many more would desert the club if it moved to the homeland of Scottish rugby?

Considering the circumstances, Head Coach Craig Levein produced astonishing feats during his four years as the man responsible for managing the playing side at Tynecastle. In 2003, he secured arguably Hearts best-ever result in European competition by leading the Maroons to a fantastic 1–0 win in Bordeaux. That was a memorable occasion for me – second only to seeing Hearts win the Scottish Cup. The day trip we had to the south of France was one of those days of perfection one rarely encounters as a Hearts supporter. A day trip to the home of vintage French wine, temperatures in the 70s and this was early November, a brilliant day in the Connemarra Bar in the heart of Bordeaux (three thousand Jambos did what only three thousand Jambos can do in the south of France – they headed to an Irish pub!), the march to the stadium, the fantastic atmosphere – and Mark de Vries scoring the winner with ten minutes to go. Inevitably, Hearts did self-destruct in the return leg at Tynecastle, going down 2–0 to go out of the UEFA Cup 2–1 on aggregate, but that day in France will never be forgotten by those who were there.

Just ten months later, Levein led Hearts to another memorable UEFA Cup victory over Sporting Braga (another fantastic day trip which goes into Gorgie folklore) which meant participation in the potentially lucrative group stages with games against Feyenoord, Schalke 04 and Ferencvaros. When it became clear that Levein would get none of this additional revenue to spend on the team, he left for Leicester City. He would soon take Hearts players Mark de Vries, Patrick Kisnorbo and, most damaging of all, Alan Maybury with him.

The fans were in despair. Our talented Head Coach had gone, some of our best players went with him and our beloved stadium was about to be turned into luxury flats. But, like Clint Eastwood riding into town in a spaghetti western, Russian businessman Vladimir Romanov then rode into Gorgie. By February 2005, he had bought a controlling interest in Hearts, the £19m debt was transferred to the Ūkio Bankas (meaning no more selling of players just to make the interest repayments) and all talk of demolishing Tynecastle ceased. Hearts were staying put!

Hearts legendary striker and now highly respected manager John Robertson left Inverness Caledonian Thistle in November 2004 to take over from Levein but, as this wasn't Romanov's appointment, his Tynecastle tenure was always going to be short-lived. Robbo gave a tearful farewell in April, barely six months after getting his dream job. Hearts finished in fifth place in the Scottish Premier League, forty-odd points behind champions Rangers and, alarmingly, eleven points behind Edinburgh's wee team. Not even a rare Hearts win at Celtic Park could save Robertson from the inevitable. Even Aberdeen finished ahead of the JTs and Hearts' reign as the 'third force' in Scottish football was at an end. The cynics opined that the Gorgie Boys were a spent force.

The search for a new manager threatened to turn into something of a soap opera. Indeed, I'm sure I saw *Coronation Street*'s Jack Duckworth linked with the job at one point. Some of the names apparently considered were dismissed as tabloid tosh but, when former England manager Sir Bobby Robson arrived in Edinburgh for talks with new Chief Executive Phil Anderton, it was the first sign that ambitions were stirring in Gorgie. However, Sir Bobby was to turn Hearts down. Next on the list was Parma coach Nevio Scala, a man with a remarkably impressive track record as a coach, and he was seriously being considered to take over in the Tynecastle hot seat.

But, when an appointment was made, it was greeted with considerable approval by the Hearts support. Former Ipswich and Derby County manager George Burley was the man given the task in late June of realising Vladimir Romanov's dream of turning Hearts into a team that would challenge the Old Firm for the championship. That was the Russian's declared statement of intent when he assumed controlling interest in February and many of the west of Scotland media hacks laughed and sneered.

George Burley's appointment came just four weeks before the SPL season kicked off. The friendly game against St Patrick's Athletic on Sunday 10 July would be the former Scotland defender's first opportunity to see his threadbare squad in action. Those of us who made the journey to Dublin stood on the small terracings of Richmond Park in the baking July heat and gave our backing to a Hearts team which looked all-too familiar from last season:

Hearts: *Gordon, Neilson, Berra, Sives, McAllister, Simmons, McFarlane, Kizys, Mikoliunas, Weir and Cesnauskis*

Hearts gave plenty of effort as usual but to say the game was scrappy is akin to saying Chris Robinson isn't universally popular. The game ended goalless and, worse still, striker Graham Weir received a serious injury that would rule him out of action for weeks.

As I met the less-than-happy Mrs Smith in Dublin's O'Connell Street after the game, I tried to placate her by stating I would have been better spending the afternoon with her on the banks of the River Liffey. Like the Hearts team, she wasn't impressed.

George Burley spoke after the game of the need to strengthen the squad and how he would be looking to bring in as many as six players before the start of the season. Such talk was alien to down-trodden Jambos but the first signs of the GB influence came little more than forty-eight hours later when Hearts crushed Bray Wanderers 5–1. Bray were a place above St Patrick's Athletic in the Eircom League so the improvement in the Hearts performance was immediate.

I had heard other Hearts managers over the course of three decades talk about bringing players in, ensuring competition for places etc., etc. Occasionally there would be a signing which would capture the imagination such as the signing of Drew Busby from the now defunct Airdrieonians in 1973. But normally the players brought in would merely strengthen the squad. George Burley, however, was true to his word. The first evidence of this was the pre-season friendly at Tynecastle against Middlesbrough on 20 July. Legendary Tynecastle stadium announcer Scott Wilson must have been aghast when he read the Hearts team sheet – 'Making his Tynecastle debut tonight is Trialist' – but there were the first signs of a team that would make the rest of Scottish football sit up and take notice.

Hearts: *Gordon, Schemmel, Pressley, Webster, McAllister, Mikoliunas, Brellier, Hartley, Skacel, Bednar and Pospisil*

A clear sign of Burley's intent to attract quality players was the appearance of Sebastian Schemmel. The Swiss fullback had been on trial at Celtic but manager Gordon Strachan wasn't convinced. After the game against Middlesbrough, neither was Burley – he didn't play for

Hearts again! There was nothing mysterious about Edgaras Jankauskas. The Lithuanian striker was a member of the FC Porto squad that won the Champions League a mere fifteen months earlier and his arrival at Tynecastle was a considerable coup. Roman Bednar, Michal Pospisil and Rudi Skacel hailed from the Czech Republic (Skacel signed on a year's loan deal from Marseille) while Frenchman Julien Brellier was once on Inter Milan's books. The excitement generated by these signings was palpable and Chief Executive Phil Anderton was quick to see the opportunity – he opened the gates of Tynecastle and let fans in for free to see this new-look Hearts team face Steve McClaren's side!

Pre-season friendlies are little more than training sessions but the new boys performed well as Hearts came from behind to secure a 1–1 draw thanks to Andy Webster's late headed equaliser. Pospisil left the field after only ten minutes through injury but it was an otherwise decent display and the near full house generated a superb atmosphere. Skacel, in particular looked highly impressive and one could sense the genuine dawn of a new era at Tynecastle. If the likes of Skacel and Jankauskas were being enticed to join the Tynecastle Revolution, the future did indeed look bright.

The final pre-season friendly came three days later at Hull, a team newly promoted to the Championship in England. With Brellier and Pospisil injured, George Burley brought in Neil McFarlane and young Calum Elliot as more than three thousand Hearts fans headed to Humberside. Edgaras Jankauskas – instantly nicknamed Eddie by the Maroon hordes – scored the only goal in the first half as Burley's charges made final preparations for the opening SPL fixture a week later.

In the multitude of previews of the season, the 'experts' had Celtic and Rangers way ahead of everyone else with Hearts being tipped as finishing in the top six come the end of the season. Hibernian and Aberdeen were the teams seen as most likely to contest third place and the coveted UEFA Cup place. The Dons had spent heavily in the summer with the likes of Barry Nicholson, Jamie Smith and Steve Lovell heading for the Granite City. Hearts' chances were instantly written off with some bookmakers giving odds of 250/1 for George's Gorgie Boys to win the league. Many media pundits were also quick to dismiss the chances of Hearts coming even close to upsetting the Glaswegian status quo. The BBC's Chick Young led the early verbal assault on George Burley's side, an opinion given little credence given Young's somewhat comical status among the station's listeners – and presenters.

'Only a fool would predict the outcome of an Old Firm game,' snarled former Aberdeen manager Willie Miller on BBC Radio Scotland's Sportsound programme a couple of years back.

Presenter Richard Gordon seized the opportunity – 'Chick?'

'I'm going for Rangers . . .'

Cue hoots of derision from the rest of the Sportsound panel as the Glaswegian made yet another faux pas. Young dismissed the new signings brought in by George Burley and declared that, if Hearts were to win the SPL this season he would buy the Hearts boss a crate of champagne. If the league flag was to fly in Gorgie for the first time in forty-six years, one would imagine champagne would not be in short supply in the Tynecastle boardroom. While Burley said all along that third place was the aim for this season, it was Young's sneering dismissive stance that irritated me and doubtless most of the rest of the Maroon Army.

It had been twenty years since anyone outside the Old Firm had won the Premier League, with genuine challenges to their domination as scarce as a Chris Robinson Appreciation Society meeting in The Diggers. Aberdeen lost the title on the last day of the season in 1990 and, while Motherwell and Hibernian both made half-hearted attempts at challenging the Glasgow twosome, no one could forget the finest Hearts team of a generation pushing the Old Firm for most of season 1997/98, before lifting the Scottish Cup at Celtic Park. But we've had two decades of the championship flag not leaving Glasgow. This is a situation which those 'journalists' who worship the Old Firm don't wish to see broken. They yearn to see Celtic and Rangers fulfil their fantasy of playing in the English Premiership and teams like Hearts are an obstacle, a hindrance to the hacks' dream of writing about their idols from the likes of Old Trafford, Stamford Bridge and Anfield. Well, fellas, believe me that ain't gonna happen and, as far as European aspirations go, you'll have to contend yourselves with a couple of trips a season to watch the Old Firm struggle against Slovakian or Cypriot opposition.

Young had the temerity to criticise George Burley for bringing in a batch of foreign players on loan, saying they surely weren't any better than any of the youngsters currently on Hearts' books. Well, with the greatest respect,

Edgaras Jankauskis, Rudi Skacel, Roman Bednar and Julien Brellier appeared to be a tad better than the likes of Graham Weir, Dennis Wyness and the now departed Joe Hamill who joined up with his mentor Craig Levein at Leicester just days into the new season.

Young's colleague, Jim Traynor, bemoaned the fact that Hearts were bringing in players on loan and that this was going against the spirit of the game. I seem to recall that Celtic won the Scottish Cup the season before (and very nearly the league title) on the back of loan-signing Craig Bellamy who would have cost £6m if the board of directors at Celtic Park had managed to prise the lid off the assorted biscuits tin to gain access to the petty cash. Bellamy ended up at Blackburn in the summer of 2005. Rangers, too, had the Greek fella Kyrgiakos on loan for the tail end of season 2004/05 and neither of the Old Firm was exactly brimming with top-class young Scots players.

Chick Young's diatribe against the Romanov Revolution was a clear sign that he and his fellow west of Scotland hacks were worried – worried that some team would, at last, challenge the Old Firm's dominance of Scottish football. But the Romanov Revolution was only just beginning. If – or should that be when? – Hearts eventually win major honours again, there will be no need for Chick Young to supply a crate of cheap plonk. It will be vintage stuff at Tynecastle.

The first game of the season is always keenly antici- pated as weeks of enduring Wimbledon, the Open Golf Championship and pro-celebrity caravanning from North Wales take their toll on the die-hard football supporter. As Hearts headed for Rugby Park to face Kilmarnock on the opening day of the league season on 30 July, the anticipation and determination were immense.

Hearts: *Gordon, Neilson, McAllister, Pressley, Hartley, Webster, Mikoliunas, McFarlane, Jankauskas, Bednar and Skacel*

Another huge Hearts support – some 3,500 – headed for Ayrshire, filling the somewhat cramped stand behind the goal. I often wonder if the stadium designers at Rugby Park forgot to enlarge the document when printing out the plans.

Eleven minutes in and the first goal of the season duly arrived – but at the wrong end for those in maroon. Youngster Steven Naismith took advantage of hesitancy in the Hearts defence and Killie were a goal to the good, much to the delight of the home fans. Cue moans and groans from some of those in the away end. Hearts always seem to struggle in the opening game of the season and this one seemed to be going the way of so many others.

But their pessimism was short-lived. Moments later, Rudi Skacel squeezed home the equaliser and Hearts didn't look back. Early in the second half, Roman Bednar stooped to nod the ball into the net to put Hearts in front before Mikoliunas added a stunning third with a fantastic volley soon after. Hearts fans celebrated but you know what happens when Jambos get too cocky . . . Gordon Greer pulled one back for Killie and we anxiously checked our watches. But, with a minute left, Jankauskas was fouled in the penalty box, Paul Hartley did his usual immaculate job from the spot and Hearts had won the opening game 4–2.

It had been a stirring encounter. Four goals away from home – the first time this had happened for two years – against a decent Killie side was impressive stuff and the new players seemed to gel instantly. For twenty-four hours Hearts sat proudly at the top of the SPL (Rangers started their season with a 3–0 win over Livingston the day after) and we lapped it up. I immediately e-mailed Jim Traynor's *Your Call* programme on BBC Radio Scotland to suggest that the SPL chiefs post the league flag to Edinburgh's west end the following Monday. Hearts had the title wrapped up!

Such was the nature of Hearts' highly impressive performance in Ayrshire, Hearts fans could hardly wait for the first league game of the season at Tynecastle – particularly as our opponents the following week were the team whose fans tell anyone who will listen that their club taught the Brazilians how to play football in the 1950s. But Hibernian were about to find out that the carnival atmosphere in Gorgie certainly wasn't to their liking.

This is how the SPL table stood on 31 July 2005:

31 JULY 2005

	P	W	D	L	F	A	Pts
Rangers	1	1	0	0	3	0	3
Hearts	1	1	0	0	4	2	3
Inverness CT	1	1	0	0	2	0	3
Celtic	1	0	1	0	4	4	1
Motherwell	1	0	1	0	4	4	1

AUGUST

Edinburgh's other team were back in European competition for 2005/06. Their opponents in the first round of the UEFA Cup were the Ukrainian side Dniepr, whom Hearts had defeated in 1991 and whose ground was not a million miles away from the site of the Chernobyl nuclear explosion in 1986 – not exactly a dream trip to the continent for our friends from across the city. But Hibernian were commemorating the fact that it was fifty years since they were the first British club to compete in the European Cup and, indeed, reached the semi-finals – a laudable achievement until you consider they played a mere six games (four of which were in Scotland as their tie against Swedish opposition was played at Firhill due to the severe winter in Scandinavia). But it's little things like these that keep the wee team's followers happy. And they were supremely confident of notching a rare win at Tynecastle on Sunday 7 August 2005 a match put back twenty-four hours to accommodate live television.

Contemplating the match beforehand in a packed Station Tavern, we looked forward to Big Eddie J. jostling with the towering figure that is Gary Smith. But, on our arrival at Tynecastle, we were shocked to discover that Jankauskas had failed a last-minute fitness test and so young Calum Elliot took his place up front.

Hearts: *Gordon, Neilson, McAllister, Pressley, Hartley, Webster, Mikoliunas, Brellier, Elliot, Bednar and Skacel*

The team ran out to a brilliant firework display as Chief Executive Phil Anderton lived up to his name of Firework Phil. And there were soon fireworks on the pitch (OK, that's enough clichés). As with most Edinburgh derbies at Tynecastle, the game started with a maroon swarm around the Hibernian goal. Roman Bednar was causing havoc but, when the opening goal duly arrived, it was Skacel, his Czech compatriot, who claimed the glory. The much-maligned Robbie Neilson eased the ball to Paul Hartley who delivered a superb pass which let Bednar through on goal. Roman's effort was blocked by the goalkeeper but Rudi Skacel followed up to scoop the ball over the line. Just twelve minutes had gone and the home fans erupted in an explosion of delirium.

Hibernian threatened soon after but it came to nothing and normal service was resumed with Steven Pressley, Andy Webster and Rudi Skacel all attempting to double Hearts' lead. The home fans had to wait until the second half until they got their wish when Stephen Glass thought he would get away with handling the ball in his own penalty box. Paul Hartley did his usual expert job with the spot kick and, at 2–0, you could almost see the white towel being thrown on to the pitch by Tony Mowbray's lot.

Minutes later the wee team's defence performed an impressive game of 'After you, Claude' to let Stephen Simmons, of all people, deliver a superb finish from just inside the penalty box to make it 3–0. Simmons had become a player often compared to the Messiah (cries of 'Jesus Christ, Simmons!' were often heard) but he went some way towards redeeming himself with his quite brilliant goal. As the Hibees fans headed for the exits, their suffering was complete when Mikoliunas drove home a fourth goal which really should have been stopped by Hibs' keeper Malkowski but, hey, what the hell? Final score Hearts 4, Hibernian 0 and memories of Mark de Vries scoring four goals in the last hammering of the Hibees – a 5–1 rout in 2002 – came flooding back (in truth they were never that far away).

Eight goals in two games and sitting top of the league, Hearts had begun the season in remarkable fashion and the fans were in raptures. I may have mentioned the dem- olition derby on more than one occasion to my colleagues of the Hibernian persuasion in the days that followed but, just in case they forgot, Hearts duly obliged by bringing out a DVD of the game within days.

Hearts' next game, however, presented an altogether more formidable obstacle. Dundee United at Tannadice is always a difficult fixture and their manager Gordon Chisholm had helped the team perform the great escape the previous season by not only dragging United away from the relegation trapdoor (sorry, that's another cliché) but leading his charges to the Scottish Cup final. This meant an unlikely place in European competition for The Arabs.

The Tannadice game was played on Sunday 14 August as United had secured a goalless draw with Mypa of Finland in the UEFA Cup preliminary round the previous Thursday. Hearts' interest in the game was astonishing. George Burley's rebuilding of the Gorgie Boys was already looking impressive and those in the media who sniped that they had yet to see the colour of Vladimir Romanov's money were left with a smattering of egg on their faces when Greek international Takis Fyssas – who had played for his country in their triumphant Euro 2004 final – became the latest big name to sign for Hearts. Hearts now had a Champions League winner and a Euro 2004 winner in their side. Hearts fans could scarcely believe it and more than five thousand of them headed to Dundee to match the size of the home support. And once more the boys in maroon had plenty to sing about.

Hearts: *Gordon, Neilson, Pressley, Webster, Fyssas, Mikoliunas, Hartley, Brellier, Skacel, Jankauskas and Bednar*

The Arabs still seemed to have their minds in Finland as Hearts continued where they had left off against Hibernian by racing into a two-goal lead before fifteen minutes had gone. Rudi Skacel's free kick was expertly delivered into the United penalty box and skipper Steven Pressley headed past a static Derek Stillie in the United goal to put Hearts a goal up after just six minutes. Six minutes later, it was 2–0. Mikoliunas saw his cross only partially cleared and picked up by Bednar. The big Czech took a touch, rolled the ball ever so slightly to his left and then fired in a powerful low shot which skimmed past Stillie. 'Easy! Easy!' chanted the Maroon hordes and, at this stage, it was.

United tried valiantly to fight back but the Hearts rearguard, with Pressley and Webster immense, stood up to the pressure. Just when it seemed certain to finish 2–0 to the JTs, Jamie McAllister linked up with Roman Bednar to set up Rudi Skacel. With the referee about to blow his whistle for full-time, Ruuuuudi duly maintained his goal-a-game record by thrashing home Hearts' third goal with a shot that struck the underside of the crossbar before hitting the net.

It ended 3–0 to Hearts and, with Rangers losing at Pittodrie, the Maroons were now clear at the top of the league – eleven goals in three games and three wins out of three. And next up was a team with a scarcely impressive record at Tynecastle – Aberdeen.

Hearts versus Aberdeen games always attract a decent crowd to Tynecastle but, with interest in the home team reaching fever pitch, it was necessary to make the game all ticket. The Dons brought down their usual large contingent of fans but their manager, the ebullient Jimmy Calderwood, helped Hearts' cause no end by declaring there was no way Hearts would remain top of the league for much longer – just the spur for Hearts to prove the man from Govan wrong as they chased win number four.

Hearts: *Gordon, Neilson, Pressley, Webster, Fyssas,
Mikoliunas, Brellier, Hartley, Skacel,
Jankauskas and Bednar*

With the Edinburgh Festival in full swing, it was a gloriously sunny August afternoon as the two clubs contesting the title of Scotland's third force did battle. Hearts started the game like a swarm of Aberdonians fighting over a fifty pence piece. Hartley, Skacel and Bednar all looked threatening. The Czech Republic duo combined to give Eddie Jankauskas the first chance of a pop at goal but the Lithuanian striker's effort skimmed just past the post. A similar combination almost had better luck minutes later but Skacel's precision cross was headed over by a less than steady Eddie.

It was only a matter of time before Hearts scored however. Aberdeen's much-lauded centre half Zander Diamond got into a fankle on the edge of his own penalty box. Step forward Rudi Skacel to intervene, turn deftly and then bury the ball past Dons keeper Ryan Esson. Cue more delirium for the home support! Soon after that, a Jankauskas header fed Bednar but Esson saved well with his feet. Further chances fell to Hartley and Skacel but half-time arrived with the league leaders just a goal to the good.

If there was one Hearts player who didn't quite match the contribution of his teammates that afternoon, it was Saulius Mikoliunas and he was replaced by former Aberdeen player Jamie McAllister for the start of the second half. But the second half began the same way as the first with Hearts on the offensive. A Paul Hartley corner was met by the head of Andy Webster but 'Smokie's' effort was less than accurate. Bednar and Skacel came close again as one began to fear that, at 1–0, Aberdeen may just come up with a smash-and-grab job and sneak a scarcely deserved equaliser.

Our fears were banished, though, when, just eight minutes from the end, substitute Michal Pospisil – on for countryman Bednar – performed an impressive overhead kick from fifteen yards to chip the ball into the net. Hearts finished out the game easy 2–0 winners. The Aberdeen support had been full of themselves at the start of the game. 'Who are ye? Who are ye?' they chanted to the home fans. By the end of the game, they had their reply. We're the league leaders, our friends in the north!

Hearts had now won four games in a row, their best start to the Premier League for more than twenty years. Three points clear at the top of the table, the predictable shout from the west of Scotland press corps was 'Yes but their real test will be against the Old Firm.'

Next up, though, for George's Boys was a trip to Hampden Park. The CIS Insurance cup-tie against Third Division amateurs Queen's Park was the ideal chance for Burley to give some 'fringe players' a chance to impress. Hearts won 2–0 thanks to a double from Eddie Jankauskas but it's fair to say it wasn't a vintage performance against The Spiders but a Hearts victory at the national stadium is such a rare event that no one fretted too much.

Hearts: *Gordon, Tierney, Wallace, Berra, Webster, Cesnauskis, Simmons, McFarlane, McAllister, Jankauskas and Pospisil*

It was back to league business the following Saturday and another game in Gorgie. Opponents Motherwell were treated by players and supporters alike with more than a hint of caution. Five times, Hearts had come up against Terry Butcher's men the previous season – and five times Hearts had failed to win. The CIS Insurance Cup semi-final in February at Easter Road saw Hearts return to their penchant of snatching defeat from the jaws of victory, having come back from two goals down against The Steelmen only to lose the tie in the final minute of extra time. But Hearts under George Burley were now a different breed.

Hearts: *Gordon, Neilson, Pressley, Webster, Fyssas, Mikoliunas, Brellier, Hartley, Skacel, Jankauskas and Bednar*

Vladimir Romanov was in the stand to witness for himself the 'revolution' and Hearts almost had the Russian on his feet after just two minutes when Paul Hartley pulled the trigger, only to see his shoot blocked by 'Well keeper Smith. The ball rebounded to Roman Bednar but the Czech Republic star ballooned his shot over the bar. After Craig Gordon denied McDonald, the unlikely figure of Robbie Neilson did a fair impression of Rab Prentice in his hey day with nifty footwork and a superb cross towards Skacel but the free-scoring midfielder was caught somewhat off balance. Steven Pressley then headed wide when the opening goal seemed inevitable and we wondered if the Motherwell jinx was going to continue under the new regime.

But, with five minutes to go until half-time, Hearts turned defence into attack with a swift counter-attack. A neat pass from Mikoliunas set up Rudi the Wonder Kid and the goal-a-game Czech maintained his record by sprinting clear and scoring with a shot from a tight angle to give the Jambos a richly deserved lead.

There then followed a remarkable incident just before the break. Skacel appeared to have sustained a bad injury following a challenge and, with the Hearts physio signalling to the bench that Rudi would have to come off, there were groans of despair around Tynecastle. But, having been stretchered to the trackside, Rudi endeared himself to the Hearts fans by hauling himself off the stretcher, snapping his shin guards back into place and signalling to the referee that he was ready to resume (much to the disgust of the physio!). The appreciation shown by the home support almost lifted the roof off the Wheatfield Stand!

There was a feeling of déjà vu at the start of the second half as Mikoliunas failed to reappear, to be replaced by Stephen Simmons. Still to score a league goal in maroon and white, early in the second half, Eddie Jankauskas nearly broke his duck with a great effort which Smith did well to save. But, with twenty minutes left to play, Eddie finally got the goal he clearly deserved. Takis Fyssas crossed into the penalty box for the former Porto hit man (yes, my little Hibernian friends, Hearts are now signing Champions League winners) to control, turn and hammer home off the underside of the crossbar.

2–0 to Hearts and victory number five looked secure although a somewhat soft penalty to Motherwell, awarded when former Jambo Jim Hamilton collapsed like a deck of cards in the penalty box, saw Richie Foran become the first opposing player to score at Tynecastle this season. The game ended 2–1 to Burley's Boys and, when legendary Tynecastle DJ – sorry, Stadium Announcer – Scott Wilson announced the full-time scores from the other games at 4.50 p.m., he invoked a reaction that certainly surprised this writer. For Hibernian had beaten Rangers 3–0 at Ibrox and normally the sound of tumbleweed blowing across the Tynecastle pitch would be heard at this point. But many Hearts fans actually cheered the result. Our superiority over the docksiders was never in doubt.

But Gorgie's finest were now five points clear at the top of the league. Twenty-two years had passed since Hearts had started a season so well. The first Saturday in September was earmarked for Scotland's forlorn quest to qualify for the 2006 World Cup but Hearts' next fixture – away to bottom of the table Livingston – was a great opportunity for Burley's men to continue their fantastic start. And it was another chance for Hearts supporters to continue to use their new buzzword with ever increasing frequency – 'Believe!'

Five games into the league season and Hearts were top of the league with a one hundred per cent record. Five points – yes, five points – clear! The Old Firm were trailing with Rangers six points behind and already getting fidgety about their trip to Tynecastle at the end of September. The sell-out crowds at Tynecastle were chanting, 'We shall not be moved!' with unbridled glee as Rudi Skacel scored yet another goal.

The smugness in Gorgie was palpable but, with each passing week, the tension increased markedly. For this is

Heart of Midlothian – a team synonymous with kicking its supporters in the teeth. But the question on every Hearts fans' lips was – 'Is this the genuine dawn of an era or another crass imitation?' The anticipation, the expectation – it didn't sit easily with this Hearts supporter. Then again, I'm of the age when I still have nightmares about East Stirlingshire visiting Tynecastle on First Division business and winning 1–0. Halloween 1981. Believe me, younger readers, it happened. Just five thousand fans at a crumbling Tynecastle as Hearts contemplated oblivion. Even the music world seemed to recognise Hearts' plight that weekend in the decade that style forgot – number one in the charts was a song called 'It's My Party and I'll Cry if I Want to' . . .

I didn't particularly enjoy the 2–1 win over Motherwell. Sure, it was Hearts' first win over Terry Butcher's side since Phil Anderton last sold a packet of Daz but the atmosphere was fraught. Craig Gordon's fabulous save in the dying moments from Willie Kinniburgh's volley earned rapturous applause from those in maroon as well as sporting claps on the back from some of the Motherwell players. But the relief on the faces of the huge number of Hearts fans at Tynecastle told its own story.

Next there was a two-week break before Hearts headed for Livingston – a game which had been switched to a Sunday to accommodate the Setanta Sports television cameras – it was surely a sign of the times when Livingston v. Hearts was deemed to be the pick of the weekend fixtures. A sign of the times too was the sight of Hearts fans queuing some considerable way down McLeod Street in order to get a ticket. Certainly the fervour surrounding

Hearts was good news for the Lithuanian bankers who doubtless looked forward to the extra revenue from live television coverage and the massive increase in ticket sales going a little way towards reducing the £19m debt which proved so unmanageable for the Bank of Scotland who demanded an annual sale of player(s) just to meet the accrued interest.

From the day Hearts won the Scottish Cup in 1998, talented player after talented player headed along Gorgie Road for the last time – Neil McCann, Davie Weir, Gary Naysmith, Colin Cameron, Antti Niemi all walked away. So, when Celtic offered a derisory amount for Paul Hartley just before the transfer window closed in August, Hearts fans bit their lips and thought, 'Here we go again.' What we didn't expect was Hearts to scoff at Celtic's offer and send Gordon Strachan back along the M8 with his tail between his short legs. Indeed Hearts offered Paul Hartley an extension to his contract and, after somewhat protracted negotiations, the former Raith Rovers and St Johnstone winger eventually signed a new three-year deal to remain in Gorgie. It was the news most Hearts fans wanted to hear and more evidence that Vladimir Romanov and George Burley meant business.

Five points clear at the top of the league and refusing to sell our best players – this wasn't the Hearts I had grown up with. But it was fantastically refreshing and I thought I was living a dream. For long-suffering Hearts fans who have been through more hard times than a Celtic Champions League flag seller, waiting for the inevitable fall to earth is akin to Scotland getting knocked out of the qualifying stages of the World Cup after failing to beat

the weakest team in the group – you fear it's going to happen but you hope it's put off for as long as possible.

I reflected at the end of this month that the real test of
this Hearts team would be twofold. First, the games
against the Old Firm – it's all very well the likes of
Aberdeen and Hibernian defeating Rangers but with
Hearts clear at the top of the SPL the Old Firm would see
their respective trips to Tynecastle as among the biggest
of the season and would raise their game accordingly.

Hearts had nothing to fear from the visit of Alex
McLeish's side – due to visit Gorgie at the end of
September – but none of us would be surprised if the game
happened to turn on a controversial decision or two in
favour of the Govan team. The SFA still hadn't forgotten
Craig Levein making fools out of them over his refusal to
pay a fine in 2003 which doubled and then quadrupled as
the SFA bigwigs flexed their muscles (Levein threatened to
take his case to the law courts before sense prevailed and
the original fine stood.) or George Foulkes standing up to
the Hampden suits following Rangers last visit to Gorgie in
March 2005.

On that occasion, Hearts were holding their Govan
rivals to a 1–1 draw when referee Hugh Dallas consulted
his assistant Andy Davis over 'an incident' in the Hearts
penalty box in the dying moments of the game. On
Davis's advice, Dallas awarded Rangers a penalty which
they duly converted and it seemed all hell had been let
loose at Tynecastle. Hearts Saulius Mikoliunas ran to
Mr Davis and barged into the official, almost knocking
him over. This resulted in an immediate red card followed
by another as the Lithuanian allegedly delivered a barrage

of abuse to the officials. It was highly impressive that Scotland's leading referee clearly understood Lithuanian swear words.

Mikoliunas was subsequently banned for five games but Hearts were far from happy about the performance of the referee and his assistant and asked the SFA to hold an inquiry into the 'integrity of the decision' to award Rangers the penalty. The media immediately saw this as Hearts accusing Mr Dallas and Mr Davis of cheating although the club strenuously denied this. The whole affair was a sorry one but Hearts showed yet again they were prepared to fight their corner against the men who purport to run the game in this country, particularly if they thought they were the victims of an injustice. If Hearts felt hard done by that night, their angst was nothing compared to that of the followers of Glasgow Celtic. Rangers won the 2004/05 league championship on the last day of a remarkable season by just two points – the two points gained by the debatable penalty on that March evening in Gorgie would prove crucial come the end of the season.

I also believed that the second real test of Hearts mettle would come when they did suffer defeat. Hearts hadn't lost a game since George Burley arrived to transform the Maroons and I stated on Jambos.net in August that it's how the team would react to a setback or two that would really show what they're made of.

George Burley knew only too well that the squad wasn't yet of sufficient quality or quantity to cope with injuries and suspensions – something that was proved when the team huffed and puffed to a 2–0 win over the amateurs Queen's Park in the CIS Insurance Cup at Hampden Park. Less than 2,500 fans headed for Hampden Park, meaning there were 50,000 empty seats. I wondered what Chris Robinson made of it all that evening.

Even though it was largely reserve players who played that night, Queen's Park manager Billy Stark – who scored for Aberdeen against Hearts in the 1986 Scottish Cup final at the same venue – stated after the game that he felt Hearts had sufficient quality in depth to push Celtic and Rangers all the way. Although George Burley clearly felt otherwise and said on more than one occasion there were areas of the team that required strengthening, the feeling in Gorgie was that, if Hearts could handle the pressure of being league leaders with their opponents subsequently raising their game against George Burley's side and Hearts were still jostling with the Old Firm for top spot in the SPL come Christmas, this may well prove to be a historic season. Neither of Glasgow's 'big two' had been convincing thus far in the season – champions Rangers had already lost to Aberdeen and Hibernian and, if Hearts were still close to the top of the league come the chimes of the New Year bells, we all believed Vladimir Romanov would come to George Burley's aid with a pot-ful of roubles. Even as the transfer window closed on the last day of August, George Burley was already compiling a list of wanted players for when the window reopened in January.

Back in 1998, Hearts manager Jim Jefferies' plea to Chris Robinson for money to buy the two players he felt was necessary for Hearts to win the league fell on deaf ears. Hearts finished third in the Premier League with the not inconsiderable consolation prize of the Scottish Cup. There seemed no reason to doubt that Romanov matched Burley's indisputable ambition – indeed, the Russian stated he expected Hearts to win the league within five years – and we began to believe that, if Hearts could make their squad stronger during the home run, then the championship dream that had burnt in the minds of Jambos for forty-six years may become reality.

Not only that, with Dundee now in the First Division and a certain Albert Kidd nowhere to be seen, we wouldn't have to worry about going to Dens Park for the final league game in May. If only we could keep this dream alive!

This is how the SPL table stood on 31 August 2005:

31 AUGUST 2005

	P	W	D	L	F	A	Pts
Hearts	5	5	0	0	15	3	15
Kilmarnock	5	3	1	1	13	8	10
Hibernian	5	3	1	1	9	5	10
Rangers	5	3	0	2	9	7	9
Celtic	4	2	1	1	10	8	7

SEPTEMBER

The first weekend in September may have been set aside for international matches but Hearts now lofty status in the game meant there was little rest for the first team players. Such was the cosmopolitan make-up of Hearts first-team squad, a dozen players were away on international duty. Critics sniped that Hearts were bringing in too many foreign players. Well, the backbone of the Scotland team, which lost narrowly to Italy in the San Siro on 7 September, was Craig Gordon, Steven Pressley, Andy Webster and Paul Hartley. Without the Hearts influence, one wondered how much lower the national team would drop in the world rankings.

Hearts' first game of the month was at Almondvale against the artists formerly known as Ferranti Thistle FC. Livingston had endured a torrid start to the league campaign under new manager Paul Lambert and the massed ranks of the Jambo Army sensed blood. Hearts were given an allocation of 6,200 tickets and, inevitably given the resurgence in interest in George Burley's men, they were snapped up quicker than Paul Hartley with a razor blade.

Setanta Sports' television deal to cover SPL games had, until the 2005/06 season, meant at least one of the Old Firm were covered every weekend. Hearts' resurgence changed the thinking of Jock Brown and co. Livingston–Hearts was seen as the game of the weekend by the television chiefs and so the game was switched to a Sunday-afternoon kick-off.

Thankfully, Livingston had the foresight to build a licensed bar under one of its stands so we spent an hour or so supping a pint or three before going round the corner to take our seats. Several rows away, one fan had attracted the attention of the press and turned the heads of his fellow fans. Vladimir Romanov showed he was a man of the people by accepting the offer of a Hearts supporters club to travel to West Lothian in their coach and sitting among their number in the stand. Forsaking his customary luxurious surroundings of the boardroom, Mr Romanov 'mixed it' with the every day supporters and another huge travelling support roared their approval.

Hearts record in West Lothian wasn't great and, when I saw that the referee was Dougie McDonald, my confidence dipped to that of the pre-Romanov era. McDonald was the referee when Hearts lost controversially to Kilmarnock at Rugby Park on 3 May 2003 (a date synonymous with bad luck for those in maroon, given the events at Dens Park in 1986) and this proved to be another afternoon that was to have huge ramifications for Hearts.

McDonald had one of those afternoons which, in the eyes of this writer, beggared belief. On that day in

May 2003, former Hearts striker Gary McSwegan, then wearing the blue and white stripes of Kilmarnock, scored the only goal of the game. Hearts' Andy Webster and Austin McCann were sent off and Craig Levein stated after the game that he lost count of the number of mistakes the referee made after ninety-seven. Cue the obligatory fine from the suits at the SFA but Levein stood his ground and took on the establishment. The fine doubled and doubled again but still the Hearts Head Coach refused to pay. The case threatened to go to the law courts until eventually a compromise was reached and Levein paid the original fine. He had taken on the SFA and won but it was something many Hearts fans feel is still being paid for today.

Hearts: *Gordon, Neilson, Pressley, Webster, Fyssas, McAllister, Brellier, Hartley, Skacel, Jankauskas and Bednar*

The game at Livingston began as so many Hearts games have began this season – with the men in maroon camped in the opposition half. We all wondered if Hearts would make it six league victories on the trot and if Rudi Skacel would maintain his goal-a-game performance in a maroon shirt. Indeed, Rudi had an early chance to do just that but his effort was off target as was Steven Pressley's as Hearts pressed Livingston so far back in their own half the Lions were almost defending on the edge of the McArthur Glen shopping complex.

We knew it wouldn't be long before Hearts opened the scoring and they did so after ten minutes. Roman Bednar had acres of room in the Livi penalty box which enabled him to turn and chip the ball to the edge of the six-yard box. Paul Hartley's header fell at the feet of Rudi the Remarkable and the Czech duly despatched the ball behind former Hearts keeper Roddy McKenzie to give Hearts the lead they richly deserved.

It was all Hearts and the gap between the teams' respective positions in the SPL was all too evident. After twenty-five minutes, Hearts doubled their lead when Bednar was fouled on the edge of the penalty box. Jamie McAllister chipped the free kick towards the back post and Andy Webster nodded past McKenzie – a goal of simplicity but expertly executed.

Livingston at last showed some urgency with Paul Dalglish proving a handful for Pressley and Webster but Hearts responded with the best goal of the afternoon ten minutes before half-time. With Livi pressing for the goal that would bring them back into the game, Hearts sprinted up the park at breathtaking pace. Eddie Jankauskas broke free and delivered a superb pass to Bednar. The striker sprinted to the edge of the Livi penalty box, looked up and drove a sublime pass across the six-yard box to give Hartley the easiest of tap-ins. Hearts were three goals to the good and further chants of 'Easy! Easy!' resonated around West Lothian.

Dalglish did pull one back for Livingston just before half-time as Hearts, to use a modern-day cliché, 'took their foot off the gas'. But, with less than half an hour of the game left, Jamie McAllister, trying to prove a point against his old team, was pulled down in the penalty box. Paul Hartley did the rest with the spot kick and the game ended

Livingston 1, Hearts 4. Burley's Boys remained five points ahead of second placed Celtic and eight ahead of Rangers. The buoyancy in Gorgie showed no sign of abating!

Six days later, Hearts faced possibly their toughest test of the season – a first ever SPL trip to the Caledonian Stadium to face the impressive Inverness Caledonian Thistle. Craig Brewster's side had given Rangers an almighty scare at the same venue a few weeks earlier and although the Highlanders were more impressive away from home, many Hearts supporters – myself included – felt this could well be the game where the one hundred percent record would go. It didn't stop more than two thousand Hearts fans setting off at dawn on Saturday 17 September to head north. Indeed, some decided to make a weekend of it and stay overnight in the Highland city after the game. They were to have yet more reasons to celebrate.

Hearts: *Gordon, Neilson, Fyssas, Pressley, Hartley, Webster, McAllister, Brellier, Jankauskas, Bednar and Skacel*

Caley Thistle were forced into one change with Dennis Wyness – on loan from Hearts – not playing against the team which paid his wages. After seeing his charges rout Livingston, George Burley went with the same starting eleven and all eyes were on Rudi Skacel to see if the mid-fielder could make it seven goals in seven games. Mid September it may have been but there was certainly no Indian summer in Inverness as the wind and rain lashed the stadium with the two thousand travelling fans doing their best to shelter from the elements.

The game began in controversial fashion. Just half a minute had elapsed when Roman Bednar was hauled to the ground as he set off on goal. Referee Mike McCurry immediately blew for a free kick and, as Thistle's Ian Black looked like he was the last man and had therefore denied Bednar a goal-scoring opportunity, we waited for the red card to be brandished by the official from Glasgow. Not so. In fact, not even a yellow card was produced and the home support heaved a collective sigh of relief.

Steven Pressley then sent a header wide before the cult hero that was Rudi Skacel fired in an impressive effort from thirty yards which Caley Thistle keeper Mark Brown did well to block. But you should not get the impression this game was as one-sided as the previous week's canter at Livingston – far from it. Caley Thistle were led from the front by their player-manager, a wily old fox whose main claim to fame was scoring the winner for Dundee United in the 1994 Scottish Cup final against Rangers. Craig Brewster had once played for Hibernian but, hey, we all do things we regret later in life (if the infamous Mrs Smith gets as far as this page, no, that wasn't one of them . . .).

Caley Thistle were enjoying more of the possession – i.e., Hearts were struggling on a tight pitch and with conditions which were monsoon-like but a characteristic of this Hearts team is that they keep producing the unexpected. After twenty-seven minutes, Rudi Skacel – come on, who else? – turned away from his marker in the penalty box before driving a low shot past keeper Brown which trundled in at the far post. 1–0 to Hearts and Skacel ran to the crowd to celebrate. Unfortunately, it was the home support that Rudi made his ill-advised gestures to and the

Czech Republic man was booked for his endeavours. Given this was the second time to date Oor Rudi had been cautioned for such behaviour this season – he had been yellow-carded after telling the Hibs support what he was going to do after scoring against them – George Burley wore a rueful look. Seven goals in seven games for Skacel but the new darling of the Hearts support was edging closer and closer to earning himself an automatic one-match ban.

Inverness went back on the offensive and it looked like they had scored a deserved equaliser five minutes before the break when Craig Dargo slipped the ball behind Craig Gordon into the net but the former Kilmarnock player was deemed to be offside, a decision not greeted with universal approval by the home support.

The second half didn't consist of a lot of football although Hearts' new Brazilian player Samuel Camazzola replaced Jamie McAllister just five minutes in. With the wind raw and the rain lashing down, 'Sammy' must have felt light years away from the sunshine of Brazil. Despite their pressure, Caley Thistle didn't give Craig Gordon too much to do and Hearts safely saw it through to the final whistle, much to the delight of the travelling support. Seven wins in seven games, Hearts were making the rest of the country sit up and take notice of the Romanov Revolution. Next up were . . . Rangers at Tynecastle.

Ah, yes, proclaimed the west of Scotland media, Hearts have started well but they've still to come up against the Old Firm. On *Scotsport* – a television programme that is Scottish Television's answer to *The Office* – pundit Andy Walker smirked that Hearts' bubble would burst when Rangers visited Gorgie the following weekend. It certainly was a game that attracted the attention of most of the United Kingdom.

Needless to say the game was a sell-out and Setanta Sports earmarked it for live TV coverage meaning a less-than-convenient 12.30 p.m. kick-off. At least it was on the Saturday but our pre-match drinking ritual was curtailed somewhat. A mark of how important the game was seen by those observers who relished the possibility of Hearts splitting the Old Firm came on BBC Radio Five Live. The station barely pays Scottish football lip service but, giving his Friday evening predictions on the station, pundit Mark Lawrenson remarked, 'Of course, the match of the day is in Scotland where league-leaders Hearts play Rangers.'

The build-up to the game was intense. Tickets were like gold dust. The media was in a frenzy, with the Glasgow hacks drooling at the prospect of the mighty Glasgow Rangers putting the young upstarts of Heart of Midlothian in their place. Not since August 1998 had Hearts defeated Rangers at Tynecastle. Joe Hamill did score the winner when Hearts beat Rangers 1–0 at Ibrox in May 2004 but, memorable though it was, that game was an end-of-season affair and meant only kudos for then Head Coach Craig Levein (although the whole country got to enjoy it as it was covered live by BBC Scotland).

But the seven-year itch for a home win against the Gers was more than an irritant. That win in '98 was Hearts' first home game since the memorable Scottish Cup triumph earlier that year but the occasion was tempered somewhat by the decision to play the game on a Sunday evening to suit SKY Television. Jim Hamilton and Stephane Adam scored the goals in a 2–1 win and we believed things couldn't get much better as a Hearts fan. In 2005, satellite television again had a say in the kick-off time but 12.30 p.m. on a Saturday was infinitely more preferable to that Sunday-evening nonsense. Over 17,000 fans swarmed to Tynecastle ready to do battle.

Hearts: *Gordon, Neilson, Fyssas, Pressley, Webster, Camazzola, Hartley, Brellier, Jankauskas, Bednar and Skacel*

Making his home debut was the Brazilian whose signing courted some controversy a few weeks earlier. Samuel Camazzola wasn't signed by George Burley. In fact, Burley had not even seen the midfield player in action. It was Vladimir Romanov who secured the services of the twenty-three-year-old Brazilian on a year-long loan deal. Burley had appeared less than enamoured with this arrangement but Camazzola had looked impressive in training and his presence on the right side of midfield in place of Jamie McAllister was designed to give Rangers' boss Alex McLeish something to think about.

Despite the early kick-off, the game began in a frenzied atmosphere. Hearts showed from the off they no longer feared the likes of Rangers and started the game the way they started all the others at Tynecastle thus far in the season – on the attack. Rudi Skacel, Roman Bednar and Eddie J. all looked in the mood as the JTs tried to rattle the champions in the opening stages. However, the best chance of the opening ten minutes fell to Rangers when former Newcastle United fullback Olivier Bernard directed his header into the ground and wide from just inside the penalty box when he really should have hit the target – not that Hearts fans were complaining.

Shortly afterwards, Skacel sprinted down the left and delivered a quite magnificent cross to Jankauskas. Eddie J. bulleted a header which was parried by the Rangers keeper for a corner. With 'There's only one Paul Hartley . . .' emanating from the noisy home support, the Scotland midfielder delivered the perfect corner kick into the six-yard area for Roman Bednar to direct his header into the net. Twelve minutes in, the score was Hearts 1, Rangers 0 and it was bedlam as the home support celebrated fervently.

Bednar immediately ran to the fans in the Wheatfield Stand, kissing the badge on his shirt. Such gestures are usually taken with more than a pinch of salt as players kissing the club badge are often off quicker than you can say loyalty bonus whenever another club offers to pay them more money but one could see the sincerity in Bednar's expression. It didn't really matter if the Czech Republic star was sincere or not – Hearts were a goal to the good and 'We shall not be moved' bellowed from the Tynecastle stands once more.

Rudi Skacel was creating havoc down the left side of midfield with his pace tying the Rangers defence in knots. Moments after Hearts went ahead, there was a great chance to double the lead. Skacel's umpteenth superb cross was met by the head of the unmarked Bednar. Unfortunately, his timing was a fraction out and his header flew over the bar but Hearts had the champions on the rack – and the home fans were loving every minute of it!

Inevitably, however, Hearts' domination wouldn't last. Past masters at dealing with troublesome opponents,

Rangers set the imposing figure of Marvin Andrews to match another run by Bednar. As Roman tried to collect a pass, Andrews lunged in with a late tackle that left Bednar in agony on the turf. It was a challenge that was to have consequences for Hearts title challenge and, although he tried to carry on, Bednar limped off the field shortly afterwards to a standing ovation from the home support. Seeing the striker in obvious distress, however, was a worrying sight for Hearts and it was confirmed a couple of days later that Bednar had suffered ligament damage which would require surgery. The big man – a vital part of the Hearts team which had taken Scottish football by storm – would be out of action for weeks. It was a bitter blow for George Burley and for the striker who had become a big favourite with the Hearts support.

An immediate indication of how big a loss the absence of Bednar would be came minutes later when the highly impressive Takis Fyssas galloped down the left wing and delivered a wonderful cross into the Rangers penalty box. With Bednar injured, there was no one there to take advantage of such great play and, in the Wheatfield Stand, we began to fret that one goal may not be enough. The ever-impressive Rudi Skacel fired in an effort that went just wide before Fyssas had to go off injured just before half-time and it looked as if the fates were conspiring against Hearts. The Greek star was replaced by Jamie McAllister as Hearts attempted to re-arrange their shape whilst trying to defend their slender lead.

Stephen Simmons had replaced Bednar up front and, while the youngster worked hard and tried manfully to rumble the Rangers rearguard, it was clear that Simmons' best position was in the middle of the park. That said, he was bundled off the ball in the penalty box just before half-time but, inevitably, referee Kenny Clark waved away appeals for a penalty.

Half-time arrived with the league leaders one goal ahead but the second half promised to be a long one – and it was. With Bednar and Fyssas off injured, Hearts had lost the initiative and Rangers, as expected, began to dominate periods of possession. They knew that defeat would leave them eleven points behind and, while it was still early in the season, having to play catch-up was not what their manager Alex McLeish wanted, especially as his team were still involved in the UEFA Champions League and the subsequent additions to an already-busy fixture list.

Although Rangers pressed hard for the equaliser, Hearts still had chances to add to their lead. Paul Hartley delivered another great cross which Jankauskas could only head over the bar. At the other end, it looked like the almost-obligatory penalty to Rangers was about to come when Hartley appeared to trip Barry Ferguson as the Rangers captain ambled into the Hearts penalty area. Referee Clark immediately blew his whistle and strode forward, reaching for a card from his top pocket. But, to the astonishment of the home support, Mr Clark awarded a free kick to Hearts and booked Ferguson for diving. Even more remarkable, in my view, was Mr Clark turning down much stronger Rangers claims for a penalty kick in the last minute when Robbie Neilson appeared to handle in the box. Changed days indeed.

The final whistle blew soon after that and there were emotional scenes among the jubilant Hearts support.

Hearts had beaten Rangers 1–0, their first Tynecastle victory over the Light Blues for seven long years and the importance of the result could not be overestimated. Hearts remained five points clear at the top of the league and, get this, eleven points ahead of the reigning Scottish champions. It had been a remarkable afternoon of a remarkable season.

It's not often the Rangers fans troop out of Tynecastle looking so dejected. Their defeat to the league leaders was their third defeat of the season – and just eight league games had been played. Some Hearts fans wore T-shirts with the declaration 'Season 2005/06 Believe!' What was noteworthy about this game was that Hearts players themselves were full of self-belief. They had passed their biggest test of the season so far with flying colours. The reigning champions knew that making up an eleven-point deficit would be a big ask.

The celebratory mood in the pub after was tempered with the realisation that Roman Bednar would almost certainly be out of action for some time. The Czech Republic forward had been a major influence on Hearts' astonishing start to the season and while his goals' tally stood at just three, his presence in a maroon shirt had been invaluable. Now Hearts faced a difficult spell without him. Bednar's countryman Michal Pospisil had also been out with injury and the good news was that he was on his way back.

However, Pospisil was some way from match fitness and, as George Burley looked ahead to Hearts' next game – a potentially tricky one at newly promoted Falkirk – a decision had to be made on who would partner

Jankauskas up front. Given his experience, Pospisil was the favourite but we wondered if the Czech Republic star would be able to last the full ninety minutes. On the other hand, young Calum Elliot had let no one down when he started at the beginning of the season and, indeed, he had given the Hibernian defence no end of trouble during the rout of the wee team back in August.

We put such quandaries to the back of our minds as we headed to the pub after the victory over Rangers. Vladimir Romanov may have had people scoffing at his dream of seeing Hearts play in the Champions League but a look at Group B of this season's illustrious competition would give everyone in Gorgie encouragement. For, alongside Arsenal, Ajax and Sparta Prague, were former Swiss amateur side FC Thun. They were the fairy tale of Swiss football – having won nothing in their one-hundred-year history, they had come from nowhere in the last decade to finish third in the Swiss First Division. With former Liverpool striker Jari Litmanen the main threat up front and former Hibs defender Allen Orman at the back, the Champions League newcomers certainly didn't lack experience. Their captain, Andres Gerber, was quoted as saying it shows that you can achieve great things in football without having a lot of money.

Such an achievement must have been music to the ears of Vladimir Romanov. If a club the size of FC Thun, a club with no history of achievement or success, could reach the so-called Holy Grail of Champions League football, then there was surely hope for Hearts. Swiss football has been dominated over the years by FC Grasshoppers of Zurich and, more recently, FC Basle. Although their dominance is not quite as strong as the Old Firm in this country, the fact that FC Thun came from nowhere to challenge for honours and take their place at the table of Europe's elite is a remarkable story – one which, if repeated in Scotland, would have the likes of Chick Young and Davie Provan choking on their fish suppers and bottles of Buckfast! The idea of Thun competing in the Champions League may well have been ridiculed by sports hacks a year ago – but it was the former amateur club who were now having the last laugh – a scenario which would not have gone unnoticed in the corridors of Tynecastle Stadium.

This is how the SPL table stood on 30 September 2005:

30 SEPTEMBER 2005

	P	W	D	L	F	A	Pts
Hearts	8	8	0	0	21	4	24
Celtic	8	6	1	1	19	9	19
Hibernian	8	5	1	2	14	8	16
Kilmarnock	8	4	2	2	17	14	14
Rangers	8	4	1	3	13	9	13

OCTOBER

Falkirk will always hold a special place in this writer's heart. It was where I saw my first Hearts game, back in October 1968. As a six-year-old living in Cumbernauld, being a junior Jambo was tough given the multitude of Celtic and Rangers fans living in Glasgow's overspill. These were the days before Burberry caps and tracksuits but the reaction of the locals was still incredulous. 'Who de ye support, pal?'

My father didn't want me poisoned by the sectarian nonsense that attaches itself to Glasgow's big two and his intention was to bring me up as a 'Falkirk Bairn', so to speak, hence my visit to Brockville. It so happened that Hearts were the visitors and I was struck by the huge numbers of visiting fans, the atmosphere they created and the sense that Hearts were the biggest club in Scotland outside of the Old Firm. The fact that the Maroons won 3−1 that day helped shape my life − for better or worse − as a Hearts supporter. I'm just thankful it wasn't Edinburgh's lesser team who were at Brockville that day.

In recent years, however, trips to Falkirk have been not so much tainted with disappointment as swamped with despair. My last visit to Brockville was in January 2003 when Hearts met Falkirk on Scottish Cup business. Falkirk were a First Division side at that time and we were confident of a relatively straightforward passage to the next round. On a bitterly cold day with driving rain and a howling wind, Hearts found themselves four goals down by half-time and echoes of a six-goal hammering at the same ground some ten years earlier came thundering back.

Nowadays, Brockville is no longer home to Falkirk FC – it's home to a supermarket. The football club has moved a few miles along the road to the imaginatively named Falkirk Stadium, a half-built symbol of twenty-first-century stadia. Hearts made their first visit there on Sunday 1 October, (yes, the game was on the Setanta Sports TV station) having won all eight league games and sitting clear at the top of the league. After the heroics against Rangers, there had been the somewhat predictable musings from Gorgie about how Falkirk would be treated with the same respect and how this game would be just as tough as a visit from the champions. The absence of the injured Roman Bednar and Takis Fyssas was a blow but, nonetheless, another huge travelling support made its way to Falkirk in expectant mood.

Hearts: *Gordon, Neilson, Pressley, Webster, McAllister, Camazzola, Hartley, Brellier, Skacel, Jankauskas and Pospisil*

The game kicked off with the Hearts anthem for this season 'We Shall Not Be Moved' ringing out from the noisy travelling fans although the home support were quick to remind us of the score the last time Hearts played Falkirk. Hearts started the game brightly with Pospisil, replacing his Czech Republic compatriot, looking lively. But there was scarcely a threat of a goal – until the twenty-fifth minute. Bairns' striker Daryl Duffy was put through on goal and, as he darted into the Hearts penalty box, Craig Gordon went to meet him – and brought him down. We swallowed hard as referee Iain Brines took the inevitable action. Having deemed Gordon to be the last man, he sent the Hearts keeper off and awarded a penalty kick to Falkirk. A double punishment, scarcely worthy of the offence (treble punishment when you consider that Gordon would then be suspended for Hearts' next league game – at Celtic Park) but Duffy did an efficient job with the spot kick and Hearts, for the first time since the opening game of the season, found themselves a goal behind.

A disconsolate Craig Gordon headed for an early shower, realising he would not be beating Henry Smith's record of one hundred consecutive goalkeeping appearances for a while yet – the game at Falkirk was Gordon's ninety-ninth – and Michal Pospisil was sacrificed as Hearts' substitute goalkeeper Steve Banks came on for his first top-team appearance, in circumstances he certainly did not wish. Down to ten men and a goal down, Hearts' fortunes deteriorated further still when injury forced the hugely influential Julien Brellier to leave the field just before half-time. Young Lee Wallace replaced him and Hearts made it to half-time without further mishap – and still only one goal behind.

The second half was merely seconds old when Duffy should have doubled Falkirk's lead but his effort was well saved by Banks. Hearts had a chance to draw level when Skacel, Jankauskas and Hartley all had efforts on goal but the danger was cleared and Falkirk breathed again. A goal did arrive – but, despairingly for Hearts, it came at the wrong end. Pressley was short with a headed pass-back to keeper Banks. The ever-dangerous Duffy nipped in and forced the goalkeeper into a fine stop – unfortunately the ball then cannoned off the onrushing Hearts skipper and trundled agonisingly over the line to put Falkirk two goals ahead. There was little over twenty minutes left and the Hearts support were silent for once. But then came a magnificent demonstration of character and guts from this Hearts team.

With just eighteen minutes left, Brazilian Samuel Camazzola floated a free kick towards the Falkirk penalty box. Steven Pressley defied the cliché that states defenders can't score sublime goals with a quite superb volley beyond Bairns keeper Glennon and Hearts had reduced the deficit to one goal. With clenched fist and a steely, determined look, Captain Marvel drove Hearts forward in search of the goal that would preserve their unbeaten run.

The final ten minutes saw Hearts entrenched in the Falkirk half as the ten men sought to salvage a point. In injury time and with Hearts' first league defeat looking inevitable, substitute Cesnauskis punted a hopeful ball into the Falkirk area. Skacel ran in, got his head to the ball only to see it ricochet off the keeper – to Steven Pressley. The captain glided the ball into the empty net to secure a vital equaliser. The final whistle blew moments later and Hearts had come back from the dead to draw 2–2. Granted, the first points of the season had been dropped as the one hundred per cent league record finally ended but the result felt like a victory and the Hearts fans reacted at the end of the game like their team had notched yet another win. They still weren't for being moved! Hearts' lead at the top of the SPL was now down to three points but the spirit in the team was evident to all. No one would find it easy to beat Hearts – even with numerical advantage!

There was now a two-week break as World Cup matters took over. Scotland had to win their final two qualifying games and hope that rivals Norway would fail to beat either Moldova or Belarus. The Scots faced a daunting trip to Slovenia but, first, had to overcome Belarus at Hampden Park. You know the script don't you? The supposedly easier of the two fixtures saw Scotland lose 1–0 to Belarus in front of nearly 50,000 agonised Scots. With Norway predictably beating the Moldovans at home it meant Scotland's final game in Slovenia was academic. Naturally, the Scots won 3–0 with Paul Hartley scoring a quite exquisite goal towards the end.

With our hopes of seeing Scotland at the 2006 World Cup Finals in Germany extinguished – in truth they were never really alight – thoughts turned back to whether Hearts could maintain their remarkable challenge at the top of the SPL. Match number ten would, perhaps, be the acid test of that challenge – Celtic at Celtic Park. Manager George Burley had a difficult build-up to the big game. With much of the Hearts squad away on international duty, Roman Bednar injured and keeper Craig

Gordon suspended, this would be a real test of Hearts acumen.

A bigger-than-usual Hearts support headed to the east end of Glasgow on 15 October. They were more expectant than normal on their visits to Glasgow and the crowd of 60,108 was Celtic's biggest of the season to date. It was the biggest game in the country by far and, as the game kicked off, the atmosphere was fervent to say the least.

Hearts: *Banks, Neilson, Pressley, Webster, Fyssas, Camazzola, Brellier, Hartley, Skacel, Jankauskas and Pospisil*

At Tynecastle, Hearts are used to kicking off and immediately thrusting into attack but, within seconds of the kick-off at Celtic Park, Michal Pospisil passed to Paul Hartley. The player who was the subject of a bid from Celtic just weeks earlier fired a ferocious shot that was palmed over the crossbar by Celtic keeper Boruc. Hearts defied the critics who sniped that they wouldn't be able to produce the goods at either Celtic Park or Ibrox and played some delightful football in the opening ten minutes. Skacel, Brellier and Pospisil were all impressive and there were some worried faces among the massed ranks of the home support.

That changed after twelve minutes, however. Nakamura combined with Sutton and Lennon to give Beattie a shot at goal. The ball took a wicked deflection and spun into the net behind Steve Banks. The home crowd roared their approval and it seemed it was going to be like another typical day at the office for Hearts in Glasgow – not for long, though.

Two minutes later, Eddie Jankauskas shot for goal but his less-than-convincing effort seemed harmless for keeper Boruc. However, the irrepressible Rudi Skacel got in about the keeper who fumbled the ball allowing Scotland's top scorer to turn and drive the ball into an empty net. It was Celtic 1, Hearts 1 and Rudi ran to the Celtic support and kissed the Hearts badge on his shirt. Inevitably, he got booked – his fourth booking in the season and all for similar offences – but you could sense from the Czech Republic star's impish grin that it was worth it to silence the Glasgow hordes!

After a Petrov appeal for a penalty was turned down, Eddie Jankauskas had a chance to put Hearts ahead but the Lithuanian striker's effort probably caused more danger for those Celtic fans in the stand behind the goal – in the top tier. Petrov and Beattie had chances just before half-time to put the Celts ahead but the interval arrived with the teams in first and second slots in the league all-square.

Celtic began to exert more pressure as the second half got underway but big Eddie J. combined brilliantly with Skacel on the hour mark, only for Rudi to see his attempt on goal blocked by the Celtic keeper. It was all Celtic in the closing stages with Hearts' keeper Steve Banks producing some impressive saves to keep the Hoops at bay. But keep them at bay he did and the final score of Celtic 1, Hearts 1 was no less than George Burley's men deserved.

Hearts remained unbeaten, remained top of the league and remained three points clear of their nearest challengers and, more importantly, proved to the rest of Scottish football – those who needed convincing – that the title challenge from the west end of Edinburgh was for real. Even the harshest of critics agreed that Hearts played well and matched Celtic. George Burley spoke eloquently – as always – after the game and Hearts now had two home fixtures – against Dunfermline Athletic and Kilmarnock – and a real chance to cement their position at the top of the league. The feel-good factor had seldom been higher.

Then, on the morning of the Dunfermline game on 22 October came the stunning news – George Burley had left the building . . .

There are certain traumatic events in your life which remain etched in your memory. You remember where you were when such a moment occurs. On a personal level, the sudden death of my father aged just fifty-eight in 1997 left me devastated for some time. On a Hearts supporting level, such traumas have been seeing a certain team winning 7–0 at Tynecastle in 1973, Hearts suffering the indignity of relegation for the first time in 1977, the transfer of John Robertson to Newcastle United in 1987, hearing the news that Wallace Mercer tried to buy Hibernian in 1990 and seeing the Scottish Cup winning team break up with alarming rapidity in 1998. Saturday 22 October 2005 saw one more trauma added to the painfully long list of the agonies of being a Hearts supporter.

All was well in the Station Tavern just before one o'clock. As we supped our pre-match pints, we were optimistic as one can ever be as a Jambo that Hearts would complete the first round of games in the SPL undefeated and remain top of the league. The television in the corner was showing the Sky Sports News channel. The sound was low but as I glanced up I saw Tynecastle Park on the screen. Sky Sports nowadays pays Scottish football scant attention, particularly on a Saturday lunchtime, so I immediately knew something was wrong. Then the the yellow tickertape displayed the news which stunned us all – George Burley had left Hearts. As bombshells go, this was one of nuclear proportions.

In thirty-seven years of following the Hearts, I've seen more ups and downs than David Blunkett's guide dog. But, just when you think you've seen it all, the living soap opera that is Heart of Midlothian Football Club comes up with something else to make you reach for the Prozac. None of us ordinary fans knew the reason(s) George Burley left Hearts in such a dramatic fashion – and hours before a vital league game. The press conference held on the Saturday evening designed to let people know what had happened was a waste of time. George Burley had left and, because of a confidentiality clause, nothing else could be added. Not much more had been added to what we knew hours earlier as we spluttered into our lunchtime pints. If Burley was sacked, surely the fans had a right to know for what reason?

Naturally the rumours were flying that evening and speculation was rife about Burley's relationship with Romanov but, if that was the reason the manager left, why on earth would he drop such a bombshell on the morning of a game? Surely he could have left it until the following Monday? The timing of this is one of the many things that irked me at the time – and still does months later. If other clubs had come in for Burley, I could only imagine they were clubs who already had managers – and this sounds underhand to say the least. As a battle weary Hearts fan of more than three decades, I should have known better than to expect my team's attempt at being the best in Scotland to be plain sailing.

Given George Burley's reputation as one of the best managers in the country, the most plausible assumption was that the former Scotland player had been dismissed. Although, when asked a couple of weeks earlier if Vladimir Romanov was telling him who to play, Burley emphatically denied this, declaring that the day this happened would be the day he walked out the door. Now he had done. Then again, I couldn't help thinking that, if the rumours were true and Vladimir Romanov was meddling with team selection, surely Burley would have waited until after the Dunfermline game before leaving?

The rumour mill was also rife with gossip about Burley's private life, the reason being that these were the same issues that saw him inexplicably leave Derby County during the summer. A story, which emerged some time after Burley's departure, suggested that Romanov had wanted his manager to seek counselling in relation to an alleged alcohol problem but that Burley refused. A story also emerged some time later that Romanov asked Burley to return but the offer was turned down flat. Whatever the reasons for this bombshell, like the bemused Hearts supporters in Gorgie on a bitter Saturday evening, the feel-good factor suddenly drifted away.

Amidst all the confusion, uncertainty and feeling of incredulity, the original reason for more than fifteen thousand Hearts supporters gathering in Gorgie that Saturday afternoon was to see their team try to maintain its unbeaten record by winning against Dunfermline Athletic.

Hearts: *Gordon, Neilson, Pressley, Webster, Fyssas, Camazzola, Brellier, Hartley, Skacel, Pospisil and Jankauskas*

After weeks of optimism, the shock news of Burley's departure instantly knocked me back into the depths of depression – so much so that I placed a couple of hard-earned pounds on a Dunfermline victory at the Tynecastle bookie, who checked and doubled checked my bet given that the Pars were 11/1 to notch a rare win in Gorgie. But, as the game kicked off, it seemed the Hearts players – who themselves had only heard the news of their manager's departure at noon – were determined to ensure they won the game as a tribute to the former Derby manager.

Some impressive, free-flowing football had the fans on their feet and the opening goal duly arrived after twenty-one minutes – inevitably from Rudi Skacel who drove in a fine twenty-yard shot for his ninth goal of the season. Two minutes later, Michal Pospisil produced an equally impressive piece of skill to chip a shot from sixteen yards into the net to double Hearts' lead and effectively seal the game.

Dunfermline showed why they faced a struggle in the SPL this season and rarely threatened. In truth, little else happened in the game until the final few minutes. First, there was an instance of real concern for the somewhat melancholy Hearts support. Paul Hartley chased after a fifty-fifty ball in his usual inimitable fashion. But the

Scotland player suddenly pulled up, clutching his thigh. The fans groaned and expected the immediate withdrawal of the former Hibernian substitute. But coach John McGlynn appeared to be asking Hartley if he was OK. Hartley signalled he was but lasted just a few minutes more before hobbling off. It was obvious he was feeling his hamstring and we suspected that, if Hearts had had a manager for this game, Hartley would not have been given a choice about staying on. Hearts were two goals to the good and, with games against Kilmarnock and Hibernian fast approaching, it seemed the obvious thing to do. Not so obvious to the Hearts' bench though.

Then, just a minute from the end, Steven Pressley was sent off for being the last man whilst committing a foul on McCunnie. If truth be told, it was a bit of a rash challenge by the Hearts skipper and this encouraged numerous conspiracy theories on the internet of the players assuming Romanov signing Ibrahim Tall would deputise for Pressley in Hearts' next game and, therefore, they would have the opportunity to show the Russian businessman that Tall was short (if you'll excuse the pun) of the quality that George Burley had expected. It was all nonsense of course as John McGlynn was put in charge of team affairs in the absence of a Head Coach and he had the not-immeasurable task of preparing the team for their second SPL fixture at Tynecastle in four days when Kilmarnock came to Tynecastle on 26 October.

Hearts: *Gordon, Neilson, Berra, Webster, Fyssas, McAllister, Brellier, Cesnauskis, Skacel, Pospisil and Jankauskas*

Our irritation on Saturday at Hartley not being immediately withdrawn after pulling up was replaced by annoyance when we discovered that the Scotland star was missing altogether for the visit of Kilmarnock. Deividas Cesnauskis took his place with young Christophe Berra replacing Steven Pressley. Another huge attendance of 16,500 turned up on a miserable, wet October evening and this was testament to a Hearts team still unbeaten and still at the top of the league. Killie would be a real test however. Manager Jim Jefferies' team had given Celtic more than a run for their money the previous Sunday with even Hoops' coach Gordon Strachan admitting his team were lucky to win 1–0.

Jefferies' personal Hearts history, of course, meant his teams were always motivated to do well at his former stamping ground and, unusually for a game at Tynecastle, it was the visitors who started better, with youngster Steven Naismith forcing Craig Gordon into a fine save just minutes into the game. But Rudi Skacel was once more making his presence felt and both he and Michal Pospisil came close to opening the scoring as the game ebbed and flowed from goalmouth to goalmouth.

Ten minutes before the break, Kilmarnock were threatening once more when Hearts turned defence into attack. Skacel got to the ball on the halfway line and burst into the Kilmarnock half before delivering a quite majestic thirty-yard cross-field pass to the on-rushing Eddie Jankauskas. The Lithuanian striker was clean through on the Killie keeper but the former Porto player's strike rate in a maroon jersey had hardly been impressive since his loan signing from FC Kaunas in the summer. We watched through our fingers but Eddie steadied himself and drilled a low shot past Killie keeper Smith to give Hearts a deserved 1–0 lead. Cue the usual chants from the home support but we were pleased to reach half-time a goal to the good. The nervous tension in the air was evident. Hearts had not been beaten for nearly six months but I sensed an anxiety in the stands that appeared to transfer itself to the players.

Hearts struggled somewhat in the second half but weren't helped by replacement referee Steven O'Reilly who had taken over from the ill Stuart Dougal. With a name like that, the more cynical Hearts fans weren't to slow to assume we would get few favours from the official – and we weren't proved wrong. Killie gave Hearts a few anxious moments as the game wore on but the Maroons really should have put such anxieties to bed. At the death, Jamie McAllister drove his shot wide of an empty goal when it seemed simpler to score but the final whistle blew soon afterwards. Hearts had extended their unbeaten run to twelve games and remained three points clear at the top of the league.

Celtic also won that evening but the biggest cheer was reserved for the news from Livingston where Rangers had stuttered once more, throwing away a two-goal lead to drop another two points in a surprise 2–2 draw. It prompted Hearts chairman George Foulkes to say afterwards that the SPL title race was now between two clubs – Hearts and Celtic. Few fans agreed with the Labour MP – particularly those of Hibernian who were gleefully relishing the visit of the league leaders to Easter Road for the next game in this astonishing season. Victory for Tony Mowbray's men would bring them to within four points of their title-chasing neighbours and would mean the championship race would have not just two, not just three but four contenders.

It seemed that tickets for the second Edinburgh derby of the season were as scarce as an invitation from the Burley family inviting Mr Romanov to spend Christmas in Ipswich. And, for once, the game lived up to the pre-match hype.

Hearts: *Gordon, Neilson, Pressley, Webster, Fyssas, Brellier, Hartley, Camazzola, Pospisil, Jankauskas and Skacel*

The match began with the usual thunderous atmosphere associated with an Edinburgh derby. Barely two minutes had passed when Steven Pressley had to leave the field after receiving a head knock and there ensued a couple of nervy moments for the Maroons before Captain Courageous resumed. Hearts had the first real chance when neat work by Fyssas found Pospisil but the Czech striker's effort was blocked by Humphrey Rudge – with a name like that he was only ever going to play for Hibs! After O'Connor went close for Hibs, Rudi Skacel produced Hearts' first real threat with a ferocious shot at goal which Hibs keeper Malkowski did well to turn away.

Skacel was the target of some bruising attention from the Hibs defence but Hearts' top scorer showed he wouldn't be bullied by coming close with another effort which stung the hands of the Hibs goalie. At the other end of the park, Derek Riordan was beginning to make his presence felt before, as half-time approached, a quite remarkable piece of refereeing from John Underhill ensued. Eddie Jankauskas clearly had the home defence worried as four Hibs players surrounded the big Lithuanian when he attempted to reach a high ball. Unfair said the referee – who promptly booked big Eddie for his troubles. Half-time arrived with the game goalless but Eddie was soon to rue his booking.

Hibs began the second period on the ascendancy but more controversy followed when Camazzola was clearly fouled by Kevin Thomson. No foul said Mr Underhill and the Hibs broke up the park and nearly opened the scoring. Cue angry jeers from the Hearts support amassed behind the goal.

Skacel and Paul Hartley then combined well with the Scotland man shooting high over the bar when the Hearts fans expected to start a triumphant dance. With under half an hour to go, the tightrope which Eddie J. had been walking since his booking finally gave way when the striker pushed Scott Brown to the ground in frustration. The referee had no choice but to produce a second yellow card. The obligatory red for two yellows followed and it was the end of the game for the former Porto striker . . . and, it transpired, the end of the game for Hearts. I won't go into the Hibs goals in any great depth but suffice to say Beuzelin and then O'Connor were given far too much space and time by the Hearts defence. Two goals were the result and Hearts' long unbeaten record was finally at an end. And at Easter Road of all places.

Celtic duly defeated Dundee United at Tannadice the following afternoon and, not only had Hearts lost their undefeated status, they were now off the top of the league on goal difference. It had been a depressing end to, quite frankly, a depressing month.

October had started with Hearts losing their one hundred per cent record at Falkirk. Next they lost their Head Coach when George Burley's departure stunned the Maroon legions. Then the unbeaten record disappeared in the worst manner possible. I was glad to see the end of October and looked forward to a steadying of the ship in November.

But Halloween 2005 had one final, shocking twist to come.

This is how the SPL table stood on 30 October 2005:

30 OCTOBER 2005

	P	W	D	L	F	A	Pts
Celtic	13	10	2	1	35	12	32
Hearts	13	10	2	1	27	9	32
Hibernian	13	9	1	3	24	13	28
Rangers	13	6	4	3	23	13	22
Kilmarnock	13	5	3	5	23	22	18

NOVEMBER

In keeping up with tradition, my wife was about to go out for the evening on Halloween and was giving me the usual grief when the sports news on the television flashed on-screen the pictures of Hearts Chief Executive Phil Anderton and Chairman George Foulkes. I didn't hear what was said thanks to the inane ramblings of my missus so I assumed it was news of a new Head Coach for Hearts. How wrong I was. Ten days after the stunning news of the departure of George Burley came the equally stunning news that Phil Anderton had left the club. George Foulkes resigned in protest at the way he perceived the way the Chief Executive had been treated. Roman Romanov, son of Vladimir, was immediately installed as Chairman and Acting Chief Executive as the storm clouds once again enveloped Gorgie Road. The question being asked by the majority of Hearts supporters that Monday evening was 'What the hell was going on at Tynecastle?'

Three of the most influential men at the country's biggest club outside of the Old Firm had left within a matter of days. Some of the media, at best suspicious of the Romanovs and at worst distrusting, were quick to pounce on the upheaval. Matters weren't helped by comments made by Foulkes to the press just hours after his departure. The feeling was that Hearts had imploded once more and it quickly became open season on the Romanovs.

Anderton's departure was the most controversial. The former Chief Executive of the Scottish Rugby Union had overseen the biggest sale of season tickets in Hearts' history. Nearly every home game was a sell-out and the pre-match atmosphere drummed up by Anderton before the home games against Hibernian and Rangers nearly blew the roof off the Wheatfield Stand. Now he and the Hearts chairman were gone. Just as we seemed to be edging back up the roller coaster after the George Burley sensation, this latest news had us plunging back down again. Some fans had gathered outside Tynecastle soon after the news broke in order to find out what was going on. The following day, Roman Romanov held court at a specially arranged press conference at Tynecastle and told the massed ranks of the press that he was taking over as chairman and the club would be looking for a new chief executive. Hearts supporters collectively shook their heads and asked what would happen next. They would receive their answer within days . . .

At times, it was easy to forget the magnificent effort of the Hearts players who had taken the club to joint top of the SPL. For the third time in a year – having taken temporary charge of the team when Craig Levein left in November 2004 and when John Robertson left in April 2005 – coach John McGlynn was left to pick up the pieces.

It had taken a supreme effort for the players to secure the win against Dunfermline Athletic just hours after George Burley's shock departure. Now, with Anderton and Foulkes also gone, the players were bound to ask what would be the next instalment of what goalkeeper Craig Gordon described as 'the Tynecastle soap opera – bigger than *Big Brother*'. McGlynn, to his credit, tried to protect his players as they prepared for their next game, at home to Dundee United on 5 November. As I headed to Gorgie on that Saturday morning, I hoped for a rocket-free Guy Fawkes Day – there had been more than enough fireworks in the past fortnight.

Hearts: *Gordon, Neilson, Pressley, Webster, Fyssas, Mikoliunas, Hartley, Brellier, Skacel, Pospisil and Elliot*

Eddie Jankauskas's indiscretion at Easter Road the previous week meant he would have to sit in the stand for the visit of Dundee United, a team that had blown hot and cold throughout the season thus far. However, their manager Gordon Chisholm had opined in the media during the week that the latest evictions from the Tynecastle House may have had an unsettling effect on the Hearts players and that his team would be ready to take advantage. Hmm, if that was the former Hibernian defender's strategy, then it was pretty much in tatters before a quarter of the game had gone.

Hearts' caretaker coach John McGlynn, who by this time may well have considered adding the words caretaker and coach to his name by deed poll, made a further change to the side which lost to the wee team by reintroducing Saulius Mikoliunas to the side in place of Camazzola and, as the game kicked off, the Lithuanian immediately set about trying convince those watching that he shouldn't be dropped from the team again. Just thirty seconds had elapsed when United's Alan Archibald felt the need to foul an already rampaging 'Miko'. Rudi Skacel delivered the free kick to the unmarked Steven Pressley but the former Dundee United defender couldn't direct his header on target and a golden chance to score in the first minute was gone. But that set the tone for the rest of the match.

Young Calum Elliot was another player trying to impress and his run set up a chance for Pospisil which wasn't taken. But, with just four minutes gone, Hearts did get the goal their early adventure deserved. Mikoliunas once again ran at the United defence and his pass found Paul Hartley on the edge of the penalty box. The Scotland man looked up before drilling the ball past United's goalie, Stillie, to give Hearts the lead. Hartley's impressive sprint to the Hearts support with his arm in the air demonstrated that this Hearts team were able rise above adversity and any apprehension felt by the fans beforehand immediately disappeared.

As Hearts continued to dominate proceedings, Elliot was the next to try his luck with a rasping shot from thirty yards. Takis Fyssas then took a leaf out of Elliot's book and tried a similar effort which Stillie tipped over the bar. A second goal just had to come and it did after twenty-five minutes. After Neilson was fouled on the right, Rudi Skacel delivered a fine cross into the penalty box from the free kick. The United defence all left it to each other and, although Pospisil tried to get a touch, Rudi's effort went straight into the net for his tenth league goal of the season. Hearts fans celebrated by chanting the name of Scotsport pundit Andy Walker, the implication from the home support being that the former Celtic striker, who had consistently dismissed Hearts league championship challenge, had an active sexual life, albeit a solitary one.

Hartley and Skacel came close once more as Hearts ended the first half of a totally one-sided affair looking for a third goal. But they had to wait until the second half for further scoring. Former Hearts star Paul Ritchie tried to clear his lines but only succeeded in hammering the ball against the on-rushing Paul Hartley. Hartley's pace saw him sprint into the United penalty box before turning a low ball across the face of the United area where the eager Michal Pospisil drove the ball home. At 3–0 for the Jambos, it seemed all over. But one thing I've learned about this damned team of ours is that it never is all over for Hearts.

United's Barry Robson ambled into the Hearts penalty area almost inviting a home defender to make a challenge. Steven Pressley duly obliged and referee Craig Thompson immediately pointed to the penalty spot. Robson himself took the kick and the former Inverness Caley Thistle man ran up and struck a thunderous shot towards goal. Craig Gordon got the full weight of his body behind the ball to deflect it back to the on-rushing Robson who tried to head the ball over the line only for the Scotland keeper to gather the ball safely. The home fans erupted in a cacophony of appreciation for the young goalkeeper. To date Hearts had conceded only one league goal at Tynecastle all season – a debatable penalty kick scored by Motherwell's Richie Foran.

As was indicated by the procession of United fans who left at that stage, the game was now all over. Pospisil did have a chance to score Hearts' fourth towards the end when he headed Mikoliunas's cross against the crossbar but the final scoreline of Hearts 3, Dundee United 0 was more than acceptable given that it had come at the end of yet another traumatic week in Gorgie.

John McGlynn paid tribute to the players afterwards but, on what turned out to be his last game in charge of the team, it's worth pointing out the superb job done by 'The Caretaker'. If ever there was a man for whom the term 'unsung hero' had been coined, it has to be John McGlynn who kept the ship afloat when first the departure of George Burley, then Phil Anderton and George Foulkes threatened to sink the good ship Heart of Midlothian. McGlynn managed to keep the players focussed throughout a difficult fortnight and, for that, the Hearts support should be forever grateful.

Hearts' win over United took them back to the top of the SPL but Celtic's victory over Falkirk twenty-four hours later saw the Hoops edge in front once more. But that weekend, the Tynecastle grapevine – akin, at times to a rolling news network for much of this season – was abuzz with the latest rumour over who would be George Burley's successor.

Hearts had spoken about a big name but the name of the latest candidate could scarcely be shorter – Rix. Graham Rix, the former Arsenal and England midfield player who had made his mark as a coach at Chelsea in pre-

Abramonvich days while helping Ruud Gullit and Gianluca Vialli coach the Blues to success. But many Hearts fans weren't happy. Their discontent was twofold. Firstly, Rix was not quite the big name that had been spoken about in the corridors of power at Tynecastle. Before his departure, Phil Anderton had spoken about top-drawer managers from across Europe 'falling over themselves' to queue for an interview for the Hearts job. Sir Bobby Robson had renewed his interest and there was apparent interest from former German international Lothar Mattheus, ex-Chelsea boss Claudio Ranieri and one time Bayern Munich coach Ottmar Hitzfeld. It's arguable whether Rix would have been at the back of that queue. Second – and most controversial – was an incident in Rix's private life in 1999 that had resulted in him serving a prison sentence and being placed on the Sex Offenders' Register for ten years. This caused considerable anger among sections of the Hearts support who believed the good name of the club would be tarnished if Rix were appointed. Speculation was rife the day after the victory over United and things weren't helped when an official club statement was issued on the club's website stating that Hearts did not wish to comment. All that did was add fuel to an already crackling fire.

The official news broke the following evening, exactly one week after the news that Anderton and Foulkes had left Tynecastle. Graham Rix was indeed the new Hearts Head Coach – at least on a short-term basis, until the end of the season.

Six years earlier Rix had had sex with a fifteen-year-old girl and had been sent to prison for six months.

It appeared, judging from the reaction that followed, that just about everyone had an opinion on this. The SFA were to conduct an investigation into whether Rix was a 'fit person to hold down such a position in Scottish football'; child protection groups declared their dissatisfaction that a sex offender was now in charge of one of Scotland's leading football clubs; and, of course, the national media declared open season on Hearts although much of the television and newspapers suggested it was Rix's lack of managerial experience which made him unsuitable rather than his conviction.

He wasn't quite the big name the Romanovs had promised. Rix's entry on the Sex Offender's Register also meant he was unable to make any contact with Hearts under-16 team. Cue torrents of moral outrage from large numbers of Hearts supporters, disbelief from sections of the press – and ridicule from supporters of Hearts rivals, chiefly those of Hibernian who, had they been able to sell the countless jokes, e-mails and text messages about Rix and his conviction, would have been able to clear the national debt. This sudden outbreak of vehement morality in Edinburgh certainly surprised this writer but the unmistakable feeling from the majority of Hearts supporters was to back the players.

Rix gave a press conference the day after his appointment became public knowledge and he came across as a knowledgeable, affable, articulate person who, having seen Hearts demolish Dundee United, was clearly impressed by the players now under his charge. My one reservation lay with the fact that the former Chelsea coach had only been given a contract until the end of the season, meaning his remit was clear – 'Deliver Hearts' first league championship for forty-six years or your situation will be reviewed.' Given the events of this astonishing season so far, this was a challenge!

The weekend of 12–13 November was yet another to have been set aside for international games and the suits at the SPL had, when compiling the fixtures back in the summer, been blessed with an optimism that few others shared – namely that Scotland would be involved in the frenzy of World Cup qualifying play-off games. As a result, there were to be no SPL fixtures that weekend but it was an important weekend in the calendar of Heart of Midlothian Football Club nonetheless.

Sunday saw the club's annual Remembrance Day Service at the Haymarket where tribute was paid to those who had given the ultimate sacrifice, fighting for their country during war. Similarities had been drawn between the current Hearts team and that of season 1914/15 in that both had won their opening eight league games. The lads of 1914, however, then enlisted to serve their country in the First World War. Seven of them never came back. They will never be forgotten and the silent tribute at the Haymarket on a cold Sunday morning in November maintained Hearts' tradition of honouring those who gave their lives so that we could be here today.

New Head Coach Graham Rix had a few days to get to know his new players before heading to Aberdeen on Sunday 20 November for another game that had been switched to accommodate the TV fellas of Setanta Sports. Despite the events of the previous few days, Hearts headed north in confident mood, particularly after the stylish way they had beaten Dundee United.

'Rix Can Fix Us the Title' proclaimed a banner among the 1,800 or so Hearts supporters at the northern outpost that is Pittodrie Stadium. On the evidence of the former Arsenal and England midfielder's first game in charge of Edinburgh's number-one championship contenders, such misplaced optimism may have disappeared quicker than a ballboy behind Craig Gordon's goal at Aberdeen.

For the first time this season, Hearts had fallen behind in points in the fight for the SPL after Celtic's victory over Rangers the day before. After managing to prise just one point from their trip to the Granite City, daylight remained between Celtic and Hearts. Graham Rix looked somewhat wary as he emerged from the Pittodrie tunnel for the start of the game but the expected hostile reception from the home support for the most part thankfully didn't materialise – the inevitable moronic and somewhat sporadic chants from the louts in the Richard Donald Stand apart. If there was no requirement for the cavalry to rescue the man now charged with delivering Hearts' first league title in forty-six years, the sight of a well-tanned, larger-than-life figure from Govan bounding towards him from the trackside may have had Rix looking for his minder. But Aberdeen manager Jimmy Calderwood's welcome was as sincere as it was warm.

It was a game that had much in common with Hearts' last appearance before the Setanta Sports television cameras back in October. Then, the Maroons had lost their one hundred per cent league record to Falkirk although a stirring fightback from two goals down and a

man down to snatch a 2–2 draw felt like a victory for
George Burley's men.

Hearts: *Gordon, Neilson, Fyssas, Pressley, Webster,*
Brellier, Skacel, Hartley, Mikoliunas,
Jankauskas and Pospisil

At Aberdeen, Hearts looked strangely out of sorts in
the opening forty-five minutes. The tactic – revived from
Craig Levein's spell in charge – of mainly launching long
balls to a big target man was, for some reason, resurrect-
ed as punt after punt was directed to Eddie Jankauskas.
Of all the aerial challenges with Russell Anderson in that
first half, I recall the big Lithuanian winning only one.
The long-ball tactic meant the normally influential Rudi
Skacel and Paul Hartley were somewhat ineffectual and it
was a surprise to no one when Aberdeen went ahead after
thirteen minutes.

The normally reliable Hearts defence made a hash of
clearing their lines and, when even the usually flawless
Julien Brellier failed to clear, the ball fell to former-Celtic
winger Jamie Smith who drove the ball low past Craig
Gordon. Cue delirium from the home support and more
moronic chanting about Hearts' Head Coach. The rest of
the first half made uncomfortable viewing for this Hearts
fan from his uncomfortable vantage point in a stadium
that used to be one of the country's finest.

Aberdeen could well have doubled their lead when
Barry Nicholson's long-range effort flew just over the bar
and, with the aforementioned Smith giving Takis Fyssas a
difficult afternoon, one wondered what kind of response

Hearts could muster. They almost grabbed what would have been an undeserved equaliser just before half-time when Mikoliunas, who had been second best to more than one fifty-fifty challenge from an Aberdeen player, at last made a contribution when he delivered a teasing cross into the penalty box which Steven Pressley glanced wide. That was about it for any noteworthy attempt at goal from a Hearts point of view in a dismal first half. It seemed certain the largely ineffectual Eddie Jankauskas would be replaced by the highly impressive Calum Elliot at the break and, as the teams returned for the second half, young Elliot was indeed out on the pitch. But Michal Pospisil had suffered an injury and it was the Czech Republic striker who had gone off meaning Big Eddie J. was reprieved for the second half.

Hearts did improve after the break – no doubt having heard a few choice words from their new Head Coach for the first time. The ball was played more to feet and, consequently, Hartley and Skacel began to exert more influence. Aberdeen seemed to sense the game was turning and adopted a more cautious approach which even manifested itself off the pitch. A rare home attempt on goal sailed over the bar, into the Richard Donald Stand and down the exits towards the burger bar. Not one ballboy or Pittodrie official made an attempt to retrieve the ball, meaning we had the extraordinary spectacle of Craig Gordon leaping over the advertising hording and into the stand to fetch the ball. Several seconds elapsed before Scotland's number-one goalkeeper returned and, as the incident wasn't included in referee Craig Thompson's report, Aberdeen had got away with a quite outrageous incident.

There was little over twenty-five minutes left to play when Jankauskas shocked the visiting support by winning a ball against Russell Anderson. Our shock turned to delight when the ball broke to Rudi the Wonder Kid whose attempt at goal deflected off Gary Dempsey, spun over the head of Aberdeen keeper Ryan Esson and into the net to give Hearts the equaliser and the vociferous travelling support something to celebrate at last. The tide had turned and suddenly Hearts attacked with menace with Hartley and Skacel causing panic in the Aberdeen rearguard. The Dons resorted to some physical challenges, one of which brought a reaction from the Hearts support alluding to the fact that Stevie Crawford used to play for the lesser team in Edinburgh and also, perhaps unfairly, questioning his parentage.

Skacel could and indeed should have won the game for Hearts when he latched on to a block from Esson but he could only fire his effort straight at the Pittodrie custodian. It summed up Hearts' day that the second rebound fell to Steven Pressley who scooped the ball into the Merkland Stand when a more delicate finish was required. Elliot then found himself clean through on goal but Esson was equal to the threat of the young Hearts forward. As the ball rolled towards Hartley, the Scotland player's attempted chip towards the gaping Aberdeen goal lacked both power and direction. Rudi Skacel then delivered a free kick which Esson tipped over and, while the game ended with Hearts dominant, there was no further goalscoring. A certain Aberdeen icon, now in charge at Celtic Park, was doubtless smiling broadly as Hearts slipped two points behind at the top of the table.

Kept back in the Aberdeen stadium for a full fifteen minutes after the final whistle (they wanted the streets cleared before letting the Hearts support loose), my attempt at engaging banter with Grampian Police's humourless officers failed miserably. I wondered if Graham Rix's explanation of two vital points lost in the north-east would have been met with a similar response from Vladimir Romanov. But there were other issues behind the former Arsenal playmaker's first game in charge of the Maroons and everyone, not least Rix himself, was relieved that a difficult first hurdle had been overcome with no serious incident – the only loss being two points which cost Hearts the chance to claim they were joint top of the league.

Another tricky away fixture was next up as Hearts travelled to Fir Park and a Motherwell side who had held something of a hoodoo over the Jambos in recent years. But with new league-leaders Celtic playing bottom club Dunfermline Athletic, Hearts knew they had to win three points to maintain the pressure on Gordon Strachan's side.

Another huge travelling support, five thousand of them, headed for Lanarkshire and it was a tribute to the Hearts fans that so many headed to Fir Park on what was a dank, miserable November day. But those who took their seats in the huge stand behind the goal received dis-appointing news when they heard the team sheets. Eddie Jankauskas had failed to recover from the injury received the previous week at Pittodrie. And, surprisingly, Michal Pospisil was nowhere to be seen. On the other hand, the sight of striker Roman Bednar on the substitutes' bench was welcome indeed but the Czech Republic player's lack of match fitness meant he would have only a limited role to play against Terry Butcher's men.

Hearts: *Gordon, Neilson, Pressley, Webster, Fyssas,*
Brellier, Hartley, Skacel, McAllister, Elliot and
Mikoliunas

All this meant that Graham Rix was forced into a major rethink on team selection. With youngster Graham Weir only returning to training after a lengthy absence, Hearts only had one fit striker and so Calum Elliot was given the lone role up front with the much-maligned Jamie McAllister brought in to the midfield. It was an awkward-looking Hearts line-up and, during another difficult first forty-five minutes, it showed. Former Jambo Jim Hamilton was the first player to strike for goal after just five minutes with a rasping effort from thirty yards but it was food and drink for Scotland's number-one goalkeeper Craig Gordon.

As in the first half at Aberdeen six days earlier, Hearts huffed and puffed but rarely threatened the home goal and it was Motherwell who came closest again when Scott McDonald – the man who scored twice in the final game of season 2004/05 to destroy Celtic's championship hopes – blasted an effort from inside the Hearts penalty box which Gordon did well to parry and even better to block Fagan's follow-up. Hearts looked distinctly uncomfortable and we wondered if they could keep the home side at bay until half-time. We got the answer we didn't want five minutes before the break when Andy Webster ran into

Hamilton and a free kick was awarded. Kerr's pass was picked up by Hamilton who delivered a low cross into the six-yard area where Motherwell's on-loan signing from Rangers, Brian McLean, tucked the ball past Gordon to put Hearts' nemesis one goal up.

For the second week running, Graham Rix had to 'have a word' with his players during the interval and, for the second week running, Hearts responded as the second half kicked off. Realising that one player up front simply wasn't working, Rix sacrificed Julien Brellier for Stephen Simmons. Simmons' natural position was in midfield but he had played up front on more than one occasion this season, scoring a memorable goal against Edinburgh's lesser team back in August. Pushing forward with more menace, Hearts still had the not-insignificant task of breaching the Motherwell defence.

The Steelmen's manager had been one of the best centre halves ever to play for, whisper it, England so his team knew a thing or two about defending. Ten minutes into the second half, however, it looked like Hearts would get the breakthrough their early play deserved. Rudi Skacel burst into the Motherwell penalty box and was crudely fouled by Richie Foran.

Referee Iain Brines immediately blew his whistle and we anticipated a penalty kick. Not so. Skacel was booked for diving and the Hearts players and officials could scarcely contain their fury. Referee Brines had failed to give Hearts justice but what his decision did do was to irk Hearts and increase their determination. With Roman Bednar replacing Mikoliunas for the final half hour, the Jambos now swarmed forward. With twenty minutes left,

Skacel had a great chance to equalise when he blasted the ball from fifteen yards out but his effort was blocked by Craigan.

As the minutes ebbed away, it looked as if Hearts were about to suffer only their second league defeat of the season. But with Pressley and Webster joining the Hearts attack as the Gorgie Boys tried to salvage a point, we crossed our collective fingers and toes. I turned to the blackened sky and pleaded with my late father that, if he wasn't spending Saturday afternoon in heaven doing anything of consequence, perhaps he could help us out here. Lo and behold, McLean, the game's only goalscorer thus far, hauled down Andy Webster in the penalty box in injury time.

This time a penalty was awarded to Hearts and Paul Hartley did his usual expert job with the spot kick to rescue a point. As referee Brines blew his whistle for the last time, our relief at seeing Hearts snatch a point turned to joy on hearing the score from Celtic Park. Bottom of the table Dunfermline Athletic had, at the risk of sounding like Tony Blackburn, quite sensationally defeated Celtic 1–0.

In the space of five minutes, we had moved from a scenario of Hearts dropping five points behind the league leaders to being just one behind. While disappointed not to have beaten Terry Butcher's men and return to the top of the SPL, I reflected later that evening in the company of a clearly disinterested Mrs Smith that even thinking about being so close to the top of the league at the end of November was normally quite alien to Hearts supporters.

A month, which had begun with the news that Phil

Anderton and George Foulkes had left Tynecastle and had continued with a controversial appointment of a replacement for George Burley, ended with Hearts just a point off the top of the league. If this was a club self-destructing as many of the media had claimed, then I couldn't wait for the tide of fortune to turn!

This is how the SPL table stood on 30 November 2005:

30 NOVEMBER 2005

	P	W	D	L	F	A	Pts
Celtic	16	12	2	2	41	13	38
Hearts	16	11	4	1	32	11	37
Hibernian	16	11	1	4	30	18	34
Rangers	16	6	5	5	24	18	23
Kilmarnock	16	6	5	5	30	26	23

DECEMBER

As my wife will tell you, I'm a bah-humbug kind of guy when it comes to Christmas and all its trappings. She thought the arrival of our first grandchild, Jack, this year would change me but, as the final month of a momentous year began, my main concern was not what to get the little fella for his first Christmas but whether Hearts would still be in championship contention come Hogmanay.

The curious logic of the SPL fixture list meant that, a month since Hearts' last home game at Tynecastle, the Gorgie Boys looked ahead to four home games in as many weeks as the party season began in earnest. First up was Livingston who headed to Gorgie on 3 December having been returned to the foot of the SPL by Dunfermline Athletics' unlikely victory in the east end of Glasgow a week earlier. With Roman Bednar now pretty close to full fitness and Eddie Jankauskas still injured, the Czech Republic striker was given a starting place in the Hearts eleven. Michal Pospisil had been given 'a word' from

Graham Rix and consequently he found a place on the substitutes' bench.

Hearts: *Gordon, Neilson, Pressley, Webster, Fyssas, Mikoliunas, Hartley, Brellier, Skacel, Elliot and Bednar*

It was a dark, miserable December day in Scotland's capital city and it had been raining for much of the preceding twenty-four hours. It said a lot for the Tynecastle ground staff that the pitch was looking in quite remarkable condition despite the almost constant downpour and the game kicked off, as Hearts home games tend to, with the Maroons flooding into attack in front of yet another impressive crowd of more than 16,500.

Rudi Skacel had been a bit off the pace at Motherwell the previous week but a couple of early flicks against Paul Lambert's men showed that Hearts' leading goalscorer was back in the mood. Just eight minutes had gone when Rudi picked up a loose pass in midfield and wasted no time in heading for the Livingston goal. He dismissed a couple of half-hearted challenges from the visitors before finding himself on the edge of the penalty box. Skacel then scorched a thunderous drive into the net, past a bemused looking Ludovic Roy in the Livi goal, and turned to the ecstatic home support in the Wheatfield Stand to milk their acclaim.

Seven minutes later, Skacel and the fans were at it again. Fit-again Roman Bednar chested the ball to Calum Elliot who immediately crossed towards the lurking Skacel. Rudi deftly controlled the ball with his chest before hammering a brilliant left-foot shot past Roy to double Hearts' lead. Soon after, Mikoliunas skipped past a couple of challenges and went close to making it three before Bednar should have scored moments later. Hearts were in easy street – or so we thought . . .

For some reason, the Maroons appeared to switch off after that frenzied opening twenty minutes. The fans, too, became quiet and the assumption appeared to be that the job against the bottom of the league side was done. Not so. Livi's McPake missed a great chance from ten yards just before half-time; then the tempo rose when the same player was lucky not to be red-carded as he seemed to swing a punch at Andy Webster. The striker seemed to sense the worst and he immediately sprinted to the tunnel as referee Alan Freeland blew for half-time. His reward for such speed of thought was to receive only a booking, a decision which, like so many others taken by Mr Freeland that afternoon, enraged the home fans.

As Hearts began the second half looking for the goal that would surely make the game safe, Bednar should have scored but drilled his fifteen-yard effort wide of the post. It was a miss which could have proved costly when, inevitably, Livingston scored on the hour mark. Julien Brellier gave the ball away cheaply and Livingston's Walker fired in a low shot from just outside the penalty box past Craig Gordon to give the irritating Livingston fan with the big drum something to bang on about.

Livi fancied their chances at snatching a point but their desperation was clearly illustrated when Vincze's throw-in eluded everyone in the Hearts penalty box and bounced beyond Craig Gordon into the net. The visitors' joy at what they thought was the equalising goal was cut short when referee Freeland pointed out that, under the laws of the game (even the laws Mr Freeland applied that afternoon), you cannot score directly from a throw-in.

There was just time for substitute Michal Pospisil to deliver a superb cross into the Livi penalty box which completely deceived Roy and bounced agonisingly off the post. The final whistle blew soon after and Hearts were back at the top of the SPL – for twenty-three hours until Celtic won at Aberdeen the following day.

In the days that followed the win over Livingston, yet another name cropped up in relation to the much-talked-about Director of Football role at Tynecastle. Former Wimbledon, Nottingham Forest and Luton Town manager Joe Kinnear was the latest name to be linked to what was fast becoming a mythical position at Tynecastle. While Kinnear said his agent had been approached by Hearts, there was no official comment from Gorgie Road. Meanwhile, Head Coach Graham Rix had more pressing matters to attend to – the visit of Inverness Caledonian Thistle at Tynecastle.

Barely a year had passed since former Caley Thistle boss John Robertson had left the Highlands to 'return home' but, of course, his stint as Hearts manager was over before the season had ended. Caley Thistle were now managed by Craig Brewster.

Brewster was forging a reputation as a coach of some ability and Caley Thistle's form in the SPL had been impressive under his tutelage. Curiously, they had been more impressive away from Inverness and, astonishingly, as they headed for the capital city on a dark but mild

December afternoon a fortnight before Christmas, they had lost just once in sixteen away games.

Hearts: *Gordon, Neilson, Fyssas, Pressley, Webster, Cesnauskis, Simmons, Hartley, Skacel, Pospisil and Elliot*

Julien Brellier's recent spate of bookings meant he was suspended for the Caley Thistle game and Stephen Simmons, who had impressed on his several appearances as a substitute this season, took his place. But it seemed a curious move by Graham Rix as Neil Macfarlane seemed the obvious choice to replace the Frenchman. The curiosity intensified when it became apparent as the game kicked off that Paul Hartley was being deployed in the holding role that Julien Brellier did so well. There was no doubt that Hartley was an able deputy but his new role clearly restricted the effectiveness of the Scotland player as Hearts toiled in midfield.

Also curious was Deividas Cesnauskis starting the game in place of Mikoliunas. If some Hearts fans were puzzled by these changes, they were aghast when the name of Roman Bednar failed to appear on the team sheet. The Czech Republic striker had failed to recover from an injury sustained against Livingston so the front two were Calum Elliot and Michal Pospisil. It all added up to what would prove to be an uneasy afternoon for those in maroon.

Hearts began the game in their now customary manner – on the attack. Buoyed up by yet another full house – it had been announced that week that Tynecastle attendances had shot up by 44% this season – an early cross by Elliot was met by the head of Stephen Simmons but his effort caused little trouble to Caley Thistle keeper Mark Brown. Inverness weathered what early storm there was and with thirty-eight-year-old Brewster causing problems for Hearts' normally rock solid defence, the Highlanders threatened more often than was comfortable for an increasingly edgy home support. Tension seemed to grip Tynecastle and, while Pospisil and Elliot worked hard, neither looked like coming even close to scoring the goal that would settle Tynecastle nerves.

Ten minutes before half-time, the opening goal should have arrived – for the team in blue, white and red. The impressive Craig Dargo left Steven Pressley for dead down the right, skipped into the Hearts penalty box and delivered the perfect cross for his player-manager. However, the normally deadly Craig Brewster sclaffed his shot wide and Hearts breathed a huge sigh of relief. The one chance of any note for the home team came shortly afterwards when Rudi Skacel robbed Proctor on the edge of the Caley Thistle penalty box but Hearts' top goalscorer's effort blazed wide. The home fans shared the anguished look on Rudi's torn face. Half-time arrived with the game goalless and, worryingly, Hearts seemingly bereft of ideas on how to change this.

The second half began in much the same manner as the first one ended. Hearts tried to mount an attack but the ultra-efficient Caley Thistle offside trap was working a treat for the Highlanders – although the home fans were less than impressed by it. Hart then forced Craig Gordon into a fine save from a free kick as news filtered through from Glasgow that Celtic had contrived to turn a one-goal half-time lead against Hibernian into a 2–1 deficit – only to launch an immediate response by scoring twice to regain the lead. Normally, news of the wee team's demise would have been greeted with cheers from those in maroon but we secretly hoped that Tony Mowbray's men would tease a draw from Glasgow's east end to help Hearts' championship bid. Well, isn't that what neighbours are for?

The fans tried to relay this news to the players and, for a while, it seemed to work as Hearts at last upped the pace. Michal Pospisil, tightly marked all afternoon, finally managed to create a bit of space for himself to deliver a superb pass to Cesnauskis. The Lithuanian bore down on goal and seemed certain to score but his fierce drive from just inside the penalty box was straight at keeper Brown and the chance was gone. Had he placed his effort either side of the keeper, Hearts would have had the lead. Craig Dargo proved a threat once more with half an hour to go when he laid the ball off to his boss but, thankfully, Mr Brewster was having one of those afternoons when nothing was going right and his effort slid past the post of Craig Gordon.

Minutes later, a frustrated Hearts were once again caught on the breakaway and Brewster fired in a brilliant half-volley from twenty-five yards which brought a stupendous save from Scotland's number-one goalkeeper who tipped the effort over the crossbar. Hearts tried manfully to turn the game their way but the introduction of Sammy Camazzola, Eddie Jankauskas and Saulius Mikoliunas did little to alter the pattern.

When Camazzola replaced Simmons, we expected

the Brazilian to take up Hartley's position in the holding role but a somewhat bemused-looking Hartley was told to stay where he was. The fans weren't slow in letting their feelings known. The game finished goalless – the first time Hearts had not won a game at Tynecastle this season and only the second time in the campaign that they had failed to score. And, for the first time this season, a few boos and jeers could be heard as referee Murray blew his whistle for the last time.

Head Coach Graham Rix tried to sound philosophical after the game, saying he could feel the tension from the fans in the stands and perhaps this had transferred itself to the players. There was no doubt this had been one of Hearts' poorest displays of the season – although this is to take nothing away from a very impressive Inverness Caledonian Thistle team who looked the likelier team to score throughout. But an afternoon, which had begun with the possibility of Hearts going back to the top of the SPL if third-placed Hibs could take something from Celtic, ended with Hearts falling further behind in the championship race.

A three-point gap had opened up – and Hearts' next opponents were reigning champions Rangers at Ibrox. The possibility of a significant gap opening up at the top of the SPL before Christmas was not the present Hearts fans wanted. And the January transfer window was still three weeks away from being unlocked.

If the build-up to the game at Ibrox wasn't quite as frenzied as the meeting between the pair at Tynecastle in September, there were the usual musings from Gorgie about being positive, looking to get the championship challenge back on track etc. etc. It had been eighteen months since Hearts had last won at Ibrox but, after years without success in Glasgow, the JTs had won both there and at Celtic Park in a year and a half and, despite recent displays, there was more expectation than usual as the Maroon hordes headed west eight days before Christmas.

Hearts: *Gordon, Neilson, Pressley, Webster, McAllister, Cesnauskis, Hartley, Brellier, Skacel, Jankauskas and Bednar*

The return of Julien Brellier from suspension was a welcome sight although the absence of Takis Fyssas – back in his homeland of Greece to witness the birth of his baby girl – was another blow for Graham Rix to contend with. The experience of Jamie McAllister, who had recovered from injury, was preferred to young Lee Wallace and Jankauskas and Bednar started the game alongside each other for the first time since Hearts had played Rangers three months earlier.

The opening twenty minutes had as much subtlety as an Audley Harrison fight. Rangers were clearly fired up for a 'must-win' match while Hearts seemed determined to show they were not going to be pushed around. This resulted in referee Mike McCurry almost wearing out his whistle in that opening period. Few chances were created but, perhaps as a taster of what was to come, Rangers came close when a Bob Malcolm free kick – yes, a Bob Malcolm free kick – was met by the head of Namouchi which brought out a fine save from Craig Gordon.

Steven Pressley almost repeated the move at the other end shortly afterwards but the Hearts skipper's header blazed over the crossbar and a real chance was gone. No doubt memories of his unhappy time at Rangers came flooding back as the home support offered ironic cheers. Andrews then missed an incredible chance for the home side by scooping the ball over the crossbar when it seemed easier to score before Craig Gordon again came to the rescue for the visitors by saving well from Burke.

But it had been poor stuff and Hearts went behind ten minutes before half-time when another Malcolm free kick was headed on by Namouchi for Lovenkrands to slip the ball past Gordon. Cue the usual songs from the home support and, even at this stage, one couldn't really see how Hearts could come back. The Maroons looked far from threatening and, once again, the once-influential Skacel and Hartley were somewhat anonymous.

The second half followed much the same pattern as the first. With twenty-five minutes remaining and Hearts as far away from a goal as President Chirac is from Tony Blair's Christmas card list, Graham Rix replaced Eddie Jankauskas with Calum Elliot and Devidias Cesnauskis with his countryman Salius Mikoliunas. Sadly, the changes made little difference and indeed Lovenkrands should have increased Rangers' lead but fired his shot into a less-than appreciative home support.

What slim chance Hearts had of rescuing a scarcely deserved point disappeared five minutes from the end when Mikoliunas went in rather crudely on home skipper Barry Ferguson and was given a straight red card. 'Miko' repeated his feat of getting sent off against Rangers from nine months earlier and, as he headed for an early bath, the embittered travelling support headed for the exits – another trip to Glasgow, another poor display.

The feeling among many Hearts fans that Saturday night was of anger and betrayal. In any other season, a nondescript 1–0 loss to Rangers at Ibrox would have been perceived as a typical Hearts display through in the west of Scotland but this season was different. Under George Burley, Hearts had been playing their best football in years with Rangers beaten at Tynecastle in September and Celtic matched man for man at Celtic Park a month after.

Although the team at Ibrox was largely the same, the football played was markedly different. The free-scoring Hearts team at the start of the season had been replaced by a more physical, cautious and uncertain team who didn't appear to understand what their new Head Coach wanted them to do. The goals had dried up as had the cre- ative juices which had previously flowed from midfield. The only thankful note from the weekend was that Celtic – who had captured the former Manchester United star Roy Keane to boost their already-strong title bid – could only draw with Inverness Caledonian Thistle the following day.

Hearts were now four points behind Gordon Strachan's men. At one point, Hearts had held a five-point lead at the top of the table. Equally concerning was that Hibernian had sneaked a typical jammy last-minute win- ner against Motherwell at Easter Road and were now just four points behind the Maroons while Rangers victory had reduced the once-yawning gap between the two to eleven points. The more pessimistic Hearts fans began to wonder if, far from winning the league, Hearts would even manage to finish in third place to secure European football the following season.

After the Rangers game, Craig Gordon spoke about Hearts having to stop the rot. Many supporters nodded in collective agreement but were already pointing accusing fingers towards the Head Coach. On his appointment just a month before, Graham Rix had been on a hiding to nothing but six points from a possible fifteen in his opening five games was not championship-challenging form. The consensus of opinion on the numerous Hearts supporters' website message boards that weekend was that the forthcoming meeting between Hearts and Celtic at Tynecastle on New Year's Day would prove pivotal.

Falkirk were next up in Gorgie on Boxing Day and this was seen as a must-win match for the Maroons. Even if the Bairns were overcome – far from a foregone conclusion given Hearts' recent form – the possibility of Celtic stretching their lead to seven points with victory on 1 January was unpalatable for many Hearts fans. Worse, in my view, was the opportunity for the wee team to close in on second place and threaten Hearts' chances of Champions League qualification. That didn't bear thinking about for this anxious Hearts fan and I was not alone in wondering what action Vladimir Romanov would take if Hearts were indeed to lose to the Hoops.

Sure, the January transfer window would enable Hearts to bring in fresh faces and it had been reported in the press that Romanov himself had been looking at players with yet another Czech Republic player, fullback

Josef Kaufman, and Liverpool reserve midfield player, Darren Potter, among those mentioned. The Potter link brought an incredulous reaction from some Hearts fans as a transfer fee of £750k was mentioned in these reports, a huge outlay for a reserve player, albeit one playing at the home of the European champions. That figure was Hearts' record fee for buying a player – the sum used to bring back John Robertson from Newcastle United in 1988 and to bring Derek Ferguson – older brother of Barry – from Rangers a year later. It said much for Hearts' recent financial fortunes that their record transfer outlay was from a decade and a half before. But, given Hearts' worrying dip in form towards the end of 2005, it looked like something drastic would be required if this incredible season was to end with some reward.

Many Hearts fans had similar Christmas wishes and, when Boxing Day arrived, having scoffed too much turkey and too many mince pies and added the pair of socks received from Auntie Margaret to the three hundred other pairs stashed away in the wardrobe, they headed for Tynecastle and the visit of a Falkirk side not without incentive to become the first visiting team to win at Tynecastle this season. For their manager was the ebullient and dyed-in-the-wool devotee of Hibernian FC John Hughes. Hearts would have to rediscover the passion if three points were to be won.

Graham Rix had spoken about having had 'a few words with the lads' in the week leading up to the game but the usual plethora of positivity emanated from the Riccarton training ground as Rix faced the press a couple of days before the game. If Hearts retained any hope of winning the league championship, it was a game they had to win.

Hearts: *Gordon, Neilson, Pressley, Webster, Fyssas, Cesnauskis, Hartley, Brellier, Skacel, Elliot and Jankauskas*

Another sell-out home support escaped the Boxing Day blues and created an atmosphere which was quite astonishing, given Hearts recent run of results. As is the norm with Hearts' performances at Tynecastle, the Maroons sprang out of the traps like a possessed greyhound. They could and perhaps should have been out of sight after the opening five minutes. Just seventy seconds had elapsed when Calum Elliot forced Falkirk keeper Glennon into a marvellous stop. Moments later, Rudi Skacel – looking hungry for goals once more – latched on to a poor pass-back but the Czech player seemed to be off balance and the chance was lost. Hearts swarmed around the Falkirk goal but there was a moment of caution when the normally reliable Takis Fyssas gave the ball away, forcing keeper Craig Gordon to make a fine save from the impressive Darryl Duffy.

The action soon returned to the other end and, in the thirteenth minute, Hearts had a brilliant chance to open the scoring. Elliot did superbly on the right to find Eddie Jankauskas lurking in the penalty box. Big Eddie controlled the ball well with his chest but his effort at goal had all the strength of the sugar off a Christmas mince pie and the Bairns keeper saved easily. That brought some groans from the home support and we prayed that this was not going to prove to be yet another of those days where Hearts pressure would count for little.

Our prayers were answered seven minutes later. As Hearts drove forward once again, Rudi Skacel caused panic in the Falkirk rearguard. With the visiting defence at sixes and sevens, the ball broke to Paul Hartley who slotted it into the net from six yards out. Hartley's impressive sprint to the adoring fans in the Wheatfield Stand illustrated the depth of feeling between the former Hibs player and the fans who still wanted to believe the impossible dream was alive.

Those fans believed even more just seconds later when Falkirk's Stephen O'Donnell, having already been booked for a crude challenge on Steven Pressley, lunged in on Julien Brellier. Referee Stuart Dougal had little alternative but to show the youngster his second yellow card quickly followed by a red. The midfield player had somewhat curiously opted to wear gloves and a short sleeve shirt but he was about to feel the heat of an early bath. It was a decision which infuriated Falkirk manager John Hughes. 'Yogi' remained a cult hero among the Hibs support (I said 'cult'), having tried manfully to marshal the Easter Road defence for a couple of seasons some years back and the emotion of seeing his Falkirk team looking as if they were about to embark on a gubbing at Tynecastle was clearly difficult for him to take.

Barely three minutes later, Hearts doubled their lead with a typically wonderful goal from Hearts' own cult hero, Rudi Skacel. Hearts top goalscorer took on a reticent Falkirk defence on the edge of the penalty area and sprinted past them before rifling a magnificent shot high into the roof of the net. Tynecastle erupted once more as Rudi danced towards his adoring audience. It was his fourteenth goal of the season and there seemed to be no stopping the midfield maestro.

Falkirk's miserable afternoon worsened just before half-time when Andy Lawrie got himself into a fankle in his own penalty box, allowing Calum Elliot to gleefully stroke the ball past Glennon for his first senior goal in a maroon shirt. The teenager had come so close to scoring throughout the season and his strength and link-up play had been impressive for one so young. When his effort at the start of the game was saved, I remarked to my mate that all he needed was a goal. When it duly arrived just before half-time, it put Hearts three goals ahead and ended the game as a contest.

We mused over our pies at half-time that, Hearts being Hearts, there was more than a fair chance that there would be no further scoring in the second half – and, for a long spell, that looked exactly how it was going to turn out. Hearts played some neat possession football but the cutting edge appeared to have been left in the dressing room at the interval. With twenty minutes left, Graham Rix replaced Jankauskas with Michal Pospisil and the fresh legs up front seemed to galvanise Hearts once more. The Czech Republic striker had been on the field for just four minutes when he met a cross from Deividas Cesnauskis and diverted his header past the stranded Glennon to put Hearts four goals to the good. Not even Hearts could throw away a four-goal lead against ten men and we relaxed, safe in the knowledge that Hearts had gained three vital points which would make facing the last remains of the turkey that bit more palatable that evening.

But there was still enough time for Calum Elliot to perform an uncanny impression of the number three bus to Dalkeith. Having waited months to see the youngster finally score for Hearts, we were treated to two goals in the same game as Elliot hit a powerful strike from the edge of the Falkirk penalty area to complete the scoring at Hearts 5, Falkirk 0.

It had been a fine afternoon that led to the much-needed restoration of the feel-good factor. News came through from the Highlands that Hibs had lost 2–0 to Inverness Caledonian Thistle and from Fife that Dunfermline Athletic had scored a last-minute penalty to snatch a 3–3 draw with Rangers. A last-minute penalty against Rangers? The referee's supervisor in the stand at East End Park must have been scribbling furiously in his notebook at the end of the game . . .

The only minor irritation of the afternoon was that Celtic scored a late winner at home to Livingston. A quick glance at the league table showed that Hearts remained four points behind the league leaders – but were now seven points clear of third-placed Hibs and thirteen ahead of Rangers.

2005 had been a memorable year. 2006 would begin with the game that everyone wanted to see – Hearts against Celtic at Tynecastle on New Year's Day. There was evidence of a Hearts team returning to form at last. A win for the Maroons would take them to within one point of the league leaders. The excitement, the tension and, of course, the hype began before they had switched off the Tynecastle floodlights on Boxing Day.

There would be fireworks at Edinburgh Castle to see in the New Year – but they would be nothing compared to the fireworks in Gorgie little more than twelve hours later.

This is how the SPL table stood on 31 December 2005:

31 DECEMBER 2005

	P	W	D	L	F	A	Pts
Celtic	20	15	3	2	50	18	48
Hearts	20	13	5	2	39	13	44
Hibernian	20	12	1	7	34	25	37
Rangers*	21	9	7	5	36	25	34
Kilmarnock	20	9	5	6	37	31	32

* Rangers played their game against Dundee United on Hogmanay – the other top four clubs played on New Year

THE CAPTAIN AND THE KEEPER

It was a bitterly cold December afternoon and the country was in holiday mood in the reflective period between Christmas and New Year. At Hearts' highly impressive training complex at Heriot-Watt University at Riccarton on the western outskirts of Scotland's capital city, the players had just finished training and, following the thumping win over Falkirk on Boxing Day, they were in positive mood ahead of the game on New Year's Day which could prove crucial to their title aspirations – the visit of Celtic to Tynecastle.

The Hearts Academy was a veritable hive of activity. Sitting in the reception area waiting to interview two major players behind Hearts incredible season – captain Steven Pressley and goalkeeper Craig Gordon – the first recognisable face I saw was someone with no Hearts connections whatsoever. Former Aberdeen striker Scott Booth was asking the somewhat harassed girl on reception duties about when Graham Rix would be available to do his interview. Booth now works as a reporter for satellite television station Setanta Sports and, as they were covering the Hearts–Celtic game live on New Year's Day, the build-up to the eagerly awaited clash had already begun. It was 1.00 p.m. and Booth was anxious as he was also booked to interview Celtic's Neil Lennon in Glasgow at 3.30 p.m. While Booth patiently waited, Sky Sports duly arrived with a cameraman and news reporter, who was less than ecstatic about having to give up his day off to interview the much-in-demand Hearts Head Coach. Coaches Stephen Frail and John McGlynn as well as Chairman Roman Romanov all scurried in and out, passing curious glances in my direction. Eventually, the imposing figure of Steven Pressley arrived and we headed for one of the many rooms at the academy to hear the views of the man I consider to be the best leader of players I have seen in a maroon jersey.

Looking back at last summer when John Robertson left and Hearts were still looking for a new manager in June, did it enter Steven's head that Hearts would be challenging for the league championship?

'I attended several meetings with Mr Romanov during the summer,' he replied, without a hint of hesitation, 'and the owner intimated throughout that time that, despite the protracted appointment of a Head Coach, he expected Hearts to be mounting a serious challenge to Rangers and Celtic. Initially, I thought we would have to rely a lot on the younger players at the club as several experienced players had left Tynecastle at the end of the preceding season. But, when George Burley arrived, the pace of acquiring quality additions to the squad accelerated.'

Burley had clearly made a favourable impression on the Hearts captain and the rest of the threadbare first-team squad but it didn't take long for the Scotland international to make an equally favourable impression on the former Derby County manager.

'When he arrived, George got the players together and asked everyone where they thought Hearts would finish in the SPL. I was the only one to say first place! Despite the lack of numbers when George first arrived, I still had faith in the team's ability. We've got some good players here and an excellent youth set-up. What's the point in not aiming as high as you can? We've set high standards at this club in the years I've been here and you've got to believe you can do it.'

With the arrival of Rudi Skacel, Roman Bednar, Edgaras Jankauskas, Julien Brellier and Michal Pospisil, closely followed by Euro–2004-winner Takis Fyssas, the standard for season 2005/06 had been set early on when Hearts raced to the top of the SPL after winning their first eight league games on the bounce.

'There was a feeling of invincibility at the start of the season,' the captain continued, 'but, even when Hearts eventually lost a game – as they were always going to do as not even the Old Firm go through an entire season undefeated – there remained a strong belief that Hearts could achieve something this season. We've already matched Celtic at Parkhead and beaten Rangers at Tynecastle. And we've beaten all the other teams in the league. If the players continue to perform to a consistent high standard and believe they can win the league, then we at least have a chance.'

Given it had been forty-six years since Hearts were last crowned champions of Scotland, did the players really believe they have a genuine chance this season?

'Of course they do.'

There was no denying the firmness in Pressley's voice.

'If Hearts don't win the league, it won't be for the lack of effort or self-belief. All the players believe they deserve to be considered genuine challengers for the championship. But the key to any success is to perform to consistently high standards and that's what the players must strive to work towards. If they can achieve that, then anything is possible.'

Speaking three days before the Hearts–Celtic top-of-the-table clash, Pressley added, 'This game may have a big bearing on the race for the league title but, no matter what the result on Sunday, nothing will be decided.'

It was a view that was to be reiterated from both Gorgie and the east end of Glasgow in the hours after the match.

As Hearts' captain, Pressley has to deal with countless interviews with the press, radio and television but, despite having never met this balding, bespectacled, overweight Hearts fan with a laptop, he was relaxed and articulate – unlike so many other footballers who resort to cliché mode whenever asked a question. He reflected on his eight years at Tynecastle, having moved to Scotland's capital city from Dundee United shortly after Hearts won the Scottish Cup in that glorious summer of 1998.

'I've enjoyed so many memorable moments,' he mused, 'most of them occurring in European games that Hearts have been involved in. We've enjoyed a fair bit of success in the UEFA Cup during my time here. Winning in Basle was a phenomenal result. Clubs bigger than Hearts couldn't win in Switzerland but we did and that was one of my proudest moments as a Hearts player. The epic victory in Bordeaux was another while the 3–2 win over Stuttgart at Tynecastle is a game which stands out because we were just one goal away from eliminating one of the top sides in Germany.'

Mention of Gordan Petric's late chance in that game to score the decisive fourth goal – and which he subsequently ballooned into the Gorgie Stand – brought a wry grin to Pressley's face. Petric was castigated by a large section of the Hearts' support during his brief spell at Tynecastle but it's a measure of Steven Pressley's professionalism that he would never stoop to criticise a fellow player.

'Results such as these show that Hearts have been a model of consistency over the past five years,' the captain added, 'which is even more impressive when you consider that, for the most part, it's been done on a shoestring budget – which is credit to Jim Jefferies, Craig Levein and John Robertson.'

With Pressley and his teammates concentrating on this incredible season, the timing of my next question had all the hallmarks of a tackle from a Hibs defender on Eddie Jankauskas – 'Where does the skipper see Hearts five years from now? Sharing the vision of Vladimir Romanov of Hearts winning the Champions League?'

'It's remarkable to be thinking about Hearts even qualifying for the Champions League. While we've already shown this season that we can compete with Celtic and Rangers, if Hearts were to firstly qualify and then make inroads in the Champions League, the club would have to attract the very top players – and that's the difficult part. When you think of clubs likely to be in the frame for winning the Champions League, you automatically think of the likes of Real Madrid, Barcelona, Juventus, the Milan clubs, Chelsea, Manchester United. Yes, FC Porto and Liverpool have defied the odds in the last couple of years but the profile of not only Hearts but Scottish football as a whole is simply not big enough to attract the highest quality of player required to win the biggest trophy in European football. It's harder than ever now for Scots clubs to do well in Europe. It's almost a quarter of a century since Aberdeen lifted the old European Cup Winners' Cup under Alex Ferguson but the format of European competition has changed dramatically since those days. That said, given Hearts' recent results against Bordeaux, Braga and Basle, I firmly believe Hearts will continue to make an impact on European football. With Mr Romanov's vision, Hearts can make an even bigger name for themselves on the continent.'

So where did Steven Pressley see Steven Pressley five years from now? Given his obvious leadership qualities, I suggested perhaps he might be managing the club.

'Well that's good of you to say so,' he laughed, 'but with any luck I still hope to be playing! I'll be thirty-seven then but I look after myself and I'm as fit as I've ever been. Perhaps I could be player-coach – used more sparingly as the years progress!'

Comparisons with another Hearts' legend from twenty years ago instantly sprung to mind. Sandy Jardine played in a similar position to Pressley and not only did Hearts come within a whisker of winning the league title, but Jardine won the Player of the Year Award in 1986 – at the age of thirty-eight.

Pressley's resolve to win a major honour with the club he now loves has never been questioned and the determination of the man was evident again as he threw a parting shot on his hopes for Hearts at the end of this incredible season. 'When you come back here to interview me next May, I hope we can do it with the SPL Championship trophy sitting just there,' he said, nodding to the space in front of the desk. 'That would be something to write about!'

It was typical of the sheer class of the man that, as we ended the interview, he asked me if I had had a good Christmas and asked about my family. When I mentioned it was my grandson's first Christmas and that, who knows, perhaps sixteen years from now Steven Pressley might be giving young Jack his first team debut, the current Hearts captain gave me a wistful look. Whatever Steven Pressley might be doing a decade and a half from now, he will still be remembered as one of the greatest ever Hearts captains.

Given the age some goalkeepers play on to in the modern game, it crossed my mind that, if grandson Jack does make his Hearts debut at the age of sixteen, what would be the chances of Craig Gordon still being between the sticks at the ripe old age of thirty-eight?

One of the best goalkeepers this writer has seen in a Hearts jersey in over thirty-five years, it's difficult to remember that Craig is just twenty-three years of age. Until you meet him and witness the ever-present smile on his fiendish good looks, you could be lulled into thinking he's still a laddie playing for the school team. In fact, when he was a laddie playing for the school team, he had already signed forms for Hearts at the tender age of twelve. What were his thoughts last summer as the numbers temporarily dwindled at Tynecastle? Being part of a Hearts team that would be challenging for the league title? Er, not quite.

'No, not at all,' said Scotland's number-one goalkeeper with admirable honesty. 'Before George Burley came, a lot of players had left and there was a lot of uncertainty. I really thought we would have to bring in a lot of young players who maybe weren't quite ready for the first team. I was thinking Hearts may be struggling to reach the top six, far less the top of the league. But the new manager made an incredible impact, brought in players of real quality and there was an immediate change.'

Having witnessed George Burley's first game in charge of Hearts – a drab goalless draw with St Patrick's Athletic in the searing Dublin heat in July – it wasn't difficult to argue with Craig's early assessment of Hearts chances for season 2005/06. But the changes made, firstly by George Burley and then by Graham Rix, had transformed Hearts from mid-table no-hopers to a team with a marvellous opportunity to qualify for the Champions League for the first time in its history.

Without displaying bravado tendencies, Gordon agreed with my humble assessment. 'Well, we have a realistic chance. Considering all that's happened in the last six months with two new managers, new players taking time to settle and the issues going on in the background, we've put ourselves in a great position. The game against Celtic on New Year's Day is a massive one. Yeah, I know it's been more than forty years since Hearts last won the league championship but all the players here believe we can achieve something this season. All I can say is that we have a chance and we've not been able to say that in recent years.'

The day before the Celtic game, Gordon would be marking his birthday with a typically quiet affair on the eve of such a big game but it's a sign of the Scotland goalkeeper's maturity that he smirked at the prospect. 'God, I'll be twenty-three,' he gasped, with a certain degree of incredulity.

My ageing brain tried desperately to search its memory bank to when I was twenty-three – ironically it coincided with the last occasion Hearts came agonisingly close to winning the league crown in season 1985/86. Before my eyes glazed over at the painful memories, I asked the current Hearts custodian between the sticks if, given he has played on some big occasions for club and country such as Bordeaux, Basle, Feyenoord and the San Siro, his preparation for these games differed any from a game on a wet November night at Fir Park.

'It's not that different. After all, football is football – you still have to play against eleven men, most of whom are trying to score against you, and, in that respect, you have to try and treat each game the same. I try to be as professional as possible in every game – be it a League-Cup game against Queen's Park at Hampden in front of a couple of thousand people or a World-Cup qualifier against Italy at the same venue before fifty thousand people. The key to it all is preparation. I try to prepare for the less glamorous games in the same way as I do for the internationals. You must remember it's your performance in these so-called smaller games that gets you noticed in the first place – if I mess up against say Albion Rovers in a Scottish-Cup tie, that wouldn't do my international chances any good.'

Wasn't he fazed when former coach Craig Levein threw him in against Bordeaux for his European debut as a twenty-year-old?

'No, I was glad the manager had confidence in my ability. I really enjoy the big occasions – the bigger the better. The Bordeaux game was a brilliant experience and whetted my appetite for more of the same.'

Hearts may have undergone a revolution under the ownership of Vladimir Romanov but they have maintained a club tradition of excellent goalkeepers. From Wembley Wizard Jack Harkness to fifties' hero Willie Duff, from Jim Cruickshank in the dark days of the 1970s to the cult figures of Henry Smith and Gordon's predecessor Antti Niemi, Hearts have nearly always had goalkeepers who have excelled. But, although he was a Hearts fan as a youngster, Craig Gordon's goalkeeping hero was a player who kept goal for Edinburgh's lesser team.

'Jim Leighton was the man who I looked up to,' Gordon stated without a whiff of irony, given that the Hearts number one is over six feet tall. 'I used to go to Easter Road to watch him and try and observe his habits. Leighton achieved so much with Aberdeen, Manchester United and Scotland and he was still at the top of his game when he played for Hibernian.'

At this point, I was going to recall Wayne Foster's winning goal for Hearts against Hibs at Easter Road in the Scottish Cup in 1994 when 'Fozzie' ran in on goal before despatching the ball though Leighton's legs for a memorable winner. But this would have been churlish on my part and I didn't want to incur the wrath of one of the best goalkeepers Hearts have ever had as he clearly still holds Leighton in high regard.

Thankfully, Gordon mentioned a few other more recognisable names as major influences on an already successful career. 'Henry Smith was another who I admired greatly and, when I first arrived at Tynecastle, Gilles Rousset was a cult hero with the Hearts support. He still is (a fact underlined when Rousset was a half-time guest at the Celtic showdown on New Year's Day and his appearance brought such an impassioned reaction from the Hearts support that they nearly brought down the old main stand twelve months prematurely). Antti Niemi was another who was a huge influence and I learned a great deal from all those players.'

So much for looking back. Where did Craig Gordon see Hearts five years hence? Fulfilling Vladimir Romanov's dream of becoming Champions League winners? He was about to answer when, with near-perfect timing, we were briefly interrupted by Roman Romanov who wanted to wish the young goalkeeper all the best for the Celtic game.

'Yeah, thanks,' offered the Scotland goalkeeper, before retuning to me. 'I think Hearts fans would be happy if the team continued to mount a strong challenge in Scotland. We've a chance of qualifying for next season's Champions League and if every season we have a chance of making it to Europe's top table then that would be something. As for winning it?' Craig offered a brief smile and a cursory glance to the departing son of the man who now controls Hearts.

As to where the Edinburgh-born keeper would be in five years there was an equally ambivalent answer.

'I've still got another eighteen months of my current contract at Tynecastle but, nonetheless, talks are on-going.* I'm happy at Hearts and, of course, I'm a Hearts fan who wants to be part of any ambitious plans for the club. But, that said, I'm ambitious on a personal level too. I would like, one day, to test myself at the very highest level. Sure, Hearts have a chance of trying to qualify for next season's Champions League but any player with ambition, whether they're a goalkeeper, centre half or striker, will tell you they want to play against the very best every week. One day I hope to play in the English Premiership against the best players in the world. I really quite fancy that.'

There is no doubt in this writer's mind that Craig Gordon would more than hold his own in the league some people (mainly the English) call the best in the world. The astonishing progress of this remarkable young man is perhaps worthy of a book on its own. Scarcely four years after being farmed out to Cowdenbeath as a raw teenager, Gordon has emerged as one of the best goalkeepers ever to play for the famous Heart of Midlothian. He has quickly established himself as the number-one number one for the Scotland national team with stirring performances against the likes of Italy, Germany and Norway. Given that many goalkeepers play on, if they maintain their fitness levels, until their late thirties it's worth reflecting that, a decade and a half

* Gordon *did* sign a new Hearts deal early in 2006.

from now, wherever Craig Gordon may be at that time, his place as one of Hearts' finest-ever goalkeepers is assured.

As I headed back into town from the frozen terrain that was the Hearts Academy, I gave thanks that Hearts not only have two inspirational Scotland internationalists driving the team forward but two level-headed and genuinely nice guys. With Steven Pressley and Craig Gordon around, it's easy to see why Vladimir Romanov believes that, for Hearts, anything is possible!

JANUARY

Like thousands of other Scots on Hogmanay, I was indulging in a whisky or two in the run up to 'the bells' at twelve midnight – except I was sampling a tottie or two purely for medicinal purposes, honestly, Your Honour. I was afflicted by a heavy cold in the last day of 2005 (I could have said flu as men never take colds – it's always the flu with us but the fact I received my flu jab a month earlier would suggest that any such claim was wrapped in self-pity.) and the alcohol intake consisted of a wee drop of whisky, boiling hot water and a couple of spoonfuls of sugar. I was keen to take to my bed as 2006 was in its infancy and hope that I would recover sufficiently to make it to Tynecastle for the New Year showdown with Celtic.

The game was originally scheduled for Hogmanay but the nice people at Setanta Sports wanted to cover the game live on TV and so the fixture was put back twenty-three hours. The upstanding people of the Lothian and Borders Police Force must have seen this decision as a double-edged sword. There was already evidence that the festive Don't Drink and Drive Campaign had not been as successful as hoped and the lack of a decent public transport system in Scotland's capital city on 1 January would surely see an increase on the number of people who had celebrated the bells twelve hours earlier running the risk of taking their car to Gorgie for the game. On the other hand, for the boys and girls in blue who were on duty on the first day of the new year, there was the prospect of substantial over-time – and given some of the incidents outside Tynecastle after the game it would prove to be hard-earned.

I stuck several tissues up my larger than average beak and gratefully accepted the offer from my mate, Gordon 'Top Man' Robertson, of a lift in his car to the game. We headed to our usual watering hole, the Station Tavern on Gorgie Road where the first signs that the day would not be a good one fell upon us. The pub was under new man-agement and with the outside of the building having received a last-minute lick of paint and the inside of the building now bereft of the usual friendly faces who knew us so well behind the bar, it felt a bit alien. As did the words Hearts and 'top-of-the-table clash'.

The atmosphere at Hearts' homes games this season was already white hot and the arrival of league-leaders Celtic and their 3,500 travelling supporters to contribute to one of Hearts' biggest home gates of the season – 17,378 – further charged an already electric atmosphere.

Hearts: *Gordon, Neilson, Pressley, Webster, Fyssas, Cesnauskis, Hartley, Brellier, Skacel, Elliot and Jankauskas*

With Roman Bednar still missing through injury, Graham Rix stuck with the same team that had thrashed Falkirk, meaning another starting place for eighteen-year-old Calum Elliot. The teenage striker had scored his first goals for Hearts in the rout over Falkirk and, to cap a fine week, he had signed a new three-and-a-half-year contract to tie one of the hottest young properties in Scottish football to Hearts.

Celtic or not, the script was already well rehearsed as the game kicked off. Hearts, keen to resume where they had left off against Falkirk on Boxing Day, beat a hasty path to the Celtic goal, eager to grab the early goal that would perhaps rattle Gordon Strachan's men. The first chance of the game, however, came at the other end when Alan Thompson sent in a cross, which worryingly saw Stilian Petrov completely unmarked at the far post. The Bulgarian should have done much better than head the ball over the crossbar from barely eight yards. Hearts, much to our relief, heeded the warning sign.

Fine play from Elliot sent Paul Hartley down the left. The Scotland star sent in a low, driven cross across the Celtic penalty box where Eddie Jankauskas was waiting. The Lithuanian seemed a tad surprised to get the ball and his effort on goal struck Hoops' player Ross Wallace before spinning into the net past keeper Boruc. Six minutes gone, 1–0 to Hearts and pandemonium at Tynecastle – it was the start we had dreamed of!

Two minutes later, bedlam! Keen to maintain the pressure, Hearts forced a corner, which the enthusiastic Rudi Skacel took. Rudi's dangerous in-swinger was met by the unmarked Steven Pressley who bulleted a header into the net and, unbelievably, Hearts were two goals up after just eight minutes. With the home support in a frenzy, Hearts continued to press forward with Elliot, Skacel and Jankauskas all threatening. Elliot, in particular, was immense and his skill had the Celtic defence in knots. Twice he set up Skacel as Hearts pushed for a third goal. Showing fantastic skill, Elliot delivered a superb cross for Rudi to finish the job but the Czech player sent his header too wide from ten yards out. Then a beautiful back-heel from the teenager sent Skacel through but Hearts' leading goalscorer, normally so deadly inside the penalty box, fired his shot straight at the Celtic keeper and another chance was lost.

Being a Hearts fan and therefore naturally pessimistic, I immediately uttered the words, 'I hope we don't regret these missed chances.' As half-time arrived and the dominant Hearts players left the field to a standing ovation, my unease was shared by more than one person alongside me in the Wheatfield Stand.

We knew Celtic would come at Hearts as soon as the second half began – and they did. But our hopes that Hearts could weather the storm increased when the hugely influential Stilian Petrov pulled up five minutes after the restart with what appeared to be a hamstring injury. He was replaced by a player who had been linked with Hearts several months earlier – Stephen Pearson. Minutes later we all wished that Hearts had gone ahead with attempts to sign the former Motherwell player when Pearson stroked home a Shaun Maloney cross past Craig Gordon to bring Celtic back into the game.

As the home support fretted, Hearts appeared to be caught between going for a third and perhaps decisive goal and keeping things tight at the back. The result was they did neither. Nakamura's effort was then parried by Gordon to Pearson who should have done better than hit the post. Maloney fired the rebound into the net but was greeted by ironic cheers from the Hearts fans as the goal was ruled out for offside. But the game turned decidedly in Celtic's favour soon after.

Maloney and Fyssas raced for the ball at the edge of the Hearts penalty box. The Greek international made a fine tackle that brought rapturous applause from the home support. What it brought from referee Ian Brines was a straight red card. To the astonishment of the home fans and the disbelief of the home players – Robbie Neilson in particular looked shell-shocked by the decision – Mr Brines deemed it not only a foul by Fyssas but also decreed he had denied Maloney a goalscoring opportunity – this despite the fact the Celtic forward appeared to be heading away from goal.

There were fifteen minutes left and we desperately hoped the Maroons would hang on to their slim lead. Graham Rix replaced Cesnauskis with young Lee Wallace while we looked to see if the ideal man for such scenarios – Neil McFarlane – would soon be joining the fray. He didn't. With three minutes to go, Hearts conceded a soft free kick on the right, Nakamura crossed and the unlikely figure of Stephen McManus headed past a static Craig Gordon to seemingly rescue a point for the league leaders.

Seconds later, another soft free kick from an almost identical spot saw another cross swing into the Hearts penalty box. With the home defence in disarray, it was young McManus again who poked the ball into the net to the joy of the delirious Celtic support in the Roseburn Stand. The game ended soon after with the barely believable scoreline of Hearts 2, Celtic 3.

Not for the first time, Hearts had snatched defeat from the jaws of victory and stunned, disbelieving Hearts fans shuffled out of Tynecastle as the Celtic hordes chanted about how much fun it was to beat the Hearts on New Year's Day.

Once again, a controversial refereeing decision had cost Hearts against the Old Firm at Tynecastle. The decision to send Fyssas off was unbelievable at the time but it beggared belief when you looked at the television replays which showed there was barely any contact between the Greek international and Shaun Maloney. To intensify matters, Celtic's Bobo Balde made a similar challenge on Cesnauskis in the first half – and received only a yellow card. Those who subscribe to conspiracy theories were giving knowing nods that signalled, 'I told you so.'

Hearts were now seven points behind Celtic although they remained six points ahead of Hibernian who drew with Kilmarnock the following afternoon. Kilmarnock it was who would visit Tynecastle the following Saturday on Scottish Cup business and a welcome break (even if it was against familiar Premier League opposition) from the grind of maintaining a league championship challenge. And, just as they had done a year earlier, Jim Jefferies' side would make it a difficult Scottish Cup day for Hearts.

Hearts: *Gordon, Neilson, Pressley, Webster, Fyssas, Mikoliunas, Hartley, Brellier, Skacel, Elliot and Jankauskas*

Graham Rix opted for a familiar starting line-up although one Lithuanian was replaced by another as Cesnauskis failed to overcome a hamstring injury and was replaced by compatriot Mikoliunas whose goal at Rugby Park on the opening day of the season remained one of the highlights of the campaign.

Hearts: *Gordon, Neilson, Pressley, Webster, Fyssas, Mikoliunas, Hartley, Brellier, Skacel, Elliot and Jankauskas*

Hearts usually start their home games in an upbeat tempo but this seemed to be missing on a cold January afternoon and there was little free-flowing football on show. Things weren't helped by another fussy performance from referee Alan Freeland who seemed to derive great pleasure in stopping the game every thirty seconds. Eddie Jankauskas almost opened the scoring for Hearts after just five minutes with a stupendous shot from twenty-five yards which smacked off the post with Killie keeper Alan Combe beaten and we sat back and awaited the expected onslaught to ensue from the home side. But it didn't materialise.

Killie were keen to make their own mark (in more ways than one, given their sometimes physical approach) with youngster Steven Naismith causing problems for Fyssas in particular. Jim Jefferies had clearly done his homework and deployed five men in midfield in an attempt to nullify the threat of Skacel and Hartley. By and large, it worked although Killie's early hard work was given scant reward when, after twenty-four minutes, Hearts took the lead. The game was fairly even at that stage but, when

Robbie Neilson hurled one of those long throw-ins that he's famous for, skipper Steven Pressley headed the ball past a motionless Combe to put Hearts one up.

Not for the first time, Hearts were inspired by their captain and there soon came an opportunity to double their lead when Mikoliunas had time and space to deliver a cross to either Eddie J. or Rudi Skacel. But the Lithuanian's delivery was hit far too hard and Killie breathed again – much to the frustration of the home support who still hadn't forgotten the number of chances that had been passed up six days earlier against Celtic. Jankauskas' injury-blighted season continued when he hobbled off just before half-time to be replaced by Michal Pospisil who then spent much of the half-time break warming up on the pitch.

Such was the short supply of skill thereafter that it became a game difficult to watch. Having spoken to numerous Kilmarnock players in the first half about some of their robust tackling, referee Freeland finally flashed a yellow card at the start of the second – to Hearts Julien Brellier. The Frenchman appeared to get in the way of the referee after the Aberdonian official had given a free kick to Killie but this was enough to see the midfield player's name go into the book.

Rudi Skacel then had a fierce drive on goal blocked on the hour mark before the home team and fans screamed for a penalty when Pospisil clearly had his shirt pulled in the penalty box. No penalty said Mr Freeland who, shortly afterwards, had to advise one of his assistants that when the ball strikes a defender and crosses the byline it normally results in a corner kick – not a throw-in.

Calum Elliot then showed why he is so highly thought

of when he displayed a neat turn of feet down the right-hand side, only for his cross to fall some way short of its intended target. That said, it almost deceived Combe before sailing past the post. With little over fifteen minutes left, the unlikely figure of substitute Jamie McAllister got on the end of Calum Elliot's cross to put Hearts two goals ahead and seemingly into the next round. The former Aberdeen player is never likely to feature high on any Hearts fan's list of all-time favourites but any player who scores one of the goals which beats Hibs in a cup final (as Jamie did when he was at Livingston) can't be all bad.

So, 2–0 to Hearts and time to bring out the cigars? Come off it – this is Hearts we're talking about. Killie's Colin Nish scrambled home a late goal meaning, not for the first time, Hearts had to hold on. The conspiracy theorists again had smirks on their faces following a couple of incidents right at the end of the game. Skacel hared down on the Killie goal and was brought down by Garry Hay. The defender was the last man and clearly denied Rudi a goalscoring opportunity. Bearing in mind what happened to Takis Fyssas a week before, surely it had to be a red card? Not so, said Alan Freeland. Yellow it was. If that decision induced feelings of disbelief it was nothing to what erupted from the home support seconds later. Wright hauled down Pospisil on the edge of the penalty box. This had to be a straight red card? Not so, said Alan Freeland. In fact, not even a yellow card.

Hearts duly clinched their place in the next round of the Scottish Cup but I was not alone in wondering what on earth had happened to the standard of Scottish refereeing. When the draw was made for the fourth round, it was another case of good news, bad news for Hearts. They received another home draw – but, once again, it was to be SPL opposition in the shape of Aberdeen.

The following Saturday it was back to league business and the short trip across the River Forth to meet Dunfermline Athletic. Or 'relegation-threatened Dunfermline' as the red-topped newspapers had renamed them. Hearts had not won a league game at East End Park for three years and had not won an away game of any description since 17 September. Would those statistics put Hearts fans off making the journey? Well, more than four thousand of them answered that question on a bright January afternoon.

Hearts: *Gordon, Neilson, Pressley, Webster, Fyssas, Mikoliunas, Hartley, Brellier, Skacel, Elliot and Pospisil*

Vladimir Romanov kept true to his word when he said Hearts would strengthen their squad during the January transfer window. Graham Rix kept the same side as the one that defeated Kilmarnock but on the substitutes' bench were two new names. Lee Johnson, a midfield player of some promise, had arrived for £50,000 from Yeovil Town while another Lithuanian, defender Nerijus Barasa arrived on loan from Romanov's other main footballing concern, FC Kaunas.

Unusually, Hearts seemed to take their time to settle in the game although the ever-eager Paul Hartley came close with a free kick early on. It was the home team who had the first real chance when Andy Tod glanced a header that went narrowly over. Tod had, once upon a time, been on loan at Tynecastle and made something of an impact when he scored with a not dissimilar header against Aberdeen at Pittodrie. It was some time ago, however.

Dunfermline's tactics were obvious – five players were deployed in midfield in an attempt to stifle Skacel and Hartley, much in the same manner as Kilmarnock had tried to seven days earlier. It seemed to work for the opening twenty-five minutes with Hearts' only attempt at goal of note an effort from Skacel which brought a fine save from home keeper McGregor. But a goal did arrive after twenty-eight minutes. Another Hartley free kick broke inside the Pars' penalty box to Calum Elliot. The youngster – named the Bank of Scotland Young Player of the Month for December – crossed into the danger area for the somewhat unlikely figure of Steven Pressley to turn the ball into the net. Young Elliot's immediate reaction in celebration was to fire the ball back into the net but, unfortunately, his shot cannoned off the goalkeeper, prompting a furious and quite unnecessary reaction from the home players – and a booking for the striker.

The goal settled Hearts and they could consider themselves unfortunate to be only one ahead at the interval. But it took only ten minutes of the second half for the Jambos to double their lead. Robbie Neilson, once more getting through a power of work, raced to the byline and cut the ball back for Michal Pospisil to thrash the ball into the net to put Hearts two goals ahead. An away-win bonus at last? Er, hang on, fellas.

Former Hearts striker Mark Burchill scored from close range minutes later and, for a brief period, the Pars exerted some pressure and threatened parity. But yet another

George Burley ponders the future at Hearts

Roman Bednar celebrates a return to goalscoring form at Livingston (Livingston 2, Hearts 3 – 5 March 2006)

Steven Pressley – arguably Hearts' best captain since John Cumming (Hearts 2, Celtic 3 – 1 January 2006)

Captain Marvel goes close to scoring
at Pittodrie (Aberdeen 1, Hearts 1 –
20 November 2005)

I'd bet my shirt I'd be Hearts' top
goalscorer – Rudi Skacel

An inspiration for Hearts and
Scotland – Paul Hartley
(Hearts 2, Celtic 3 – 1 January 2006)

The best goalkeeper in Britain –
Craig Gordon

Julien Brellier tries to avoid a yellow
card against Partick Thistle – he failed
(Hearts 2, Partick Thistle 1 –
25 February 2006)

Andy Webster – the rock in the
Hearts defence (Celtic 1, Hearts 1 –
15 October 2005)

Calum Elliot scores against Aberdeen
– much to Hartley's delight (Hearts
1, Aberdeen 2 – 11 February 2006)

Pressley brings Hearts back from the
dead at Falkirk (Falkirk 2, Hearts 2 –
2 October 2005)

Vladimir Romanov spells out his
five-year plan

Roman Romanov, Vladimir's son, took
over from George Foulkes as Chairman

Eddie Jankauskas scores against Celtic (Hearts 2, Celtic 3 – 1 January 2006)

Roman Bednar heads home against Rangers – he would suffer a serious injury minutes later (Hearts 1, Rangers 0 – 24 September 2005)

Graham Rix feeling the pressure

The Job Centre's down there, mate – Jim Duffy tries to help his friend

Craig Gordon – a picture of agility (Hibernian 2, Hearts 0 – 29 October 2005)

Rudi scores against the wee team at Tynecastle (Hearts 4, Hibernian 1 –
28 January 2006)

Hat-trick hero Paul Hartley celebrates in the Scottish Cup semi-final demolition derby over Hibernian (Hearts 4, Hibernian 0 – 2 April 2006)

Acting Head Coach Valdas Ivanauskas – only four goals against Hibernian? Not enough, mate (Hearts 4, Hibernian 0 – 2 April 2006)

Hearts players perform their victory huddle in front of the huge Hibernian support at Hampden (Hearts 4, Hibernian 0 – 2 April 2006)

Robbie Neilson holds off James Grady during the final of the Scottish Cup at Hampden. Neilson went on to make a crucial tackle to deny Gretna a certain goal. (Hearts 1, Gretna 1, Hearts 4, Gretna 2 on penalties – 13 May 2006)

In an action-packed cup final, Gretna played some amazing football but Hearts won on penalties. Here, Captain Marvel, Steven Pressley, proudly lifts the cup.

Around 100,000 Hearts fans took to the streets of the capital to welcome the cup winners home. Pressley admitted he had to hold back the tears as the open-top bus made its way to Tynecastle.

Paul Hartley free kick provided danger for the home defence and Pospisil sent a glancing header past McGregor to make the game safe for Hearts at 3–1. Inevitably, the enigmatic Rudi Skacel couldn't let the day pass without adding his name to the score sheet and, with nine minutes left, he latched on to a through pass from the superb Julien Brellier before tucking the ball behind McGregor.

At 4–1 to Hearts, there was still time for a quite outrageous piece of skill from Hearts' leading goalscorer when the Czech midfield star performed a flick of Brazilian standards from twenty-five yards out which spun over the head of the goalkeeper and smacked off both the crossbar and post. By now, new boys Barasa and Johnson had came on as second-half substitutes and a near-perfect day was complete when news came through that Hibernian had lost 2–1 to Aberdeen at Easter Road. I say a near-perfect day because Celtic had fended off a spirited Kilmarnock fightback to win 4–2 in Glasgow and therefore maintained their seven-point lead. But the feeling among the travelling Maroon Army was that this was Hearts' best performance in weeks – if they could maintain this until the end of the season, perhaps the league title would not seem the distant trophy it seemed at present.

A player who played an integral part in the last Hearts team that challenged for the league championship in 1998 was once again paraded in a Hearts jersey as he returned to the place where he belonged – and some say should never have left. Neil McCann, wing wizard and hero of the Hearts support that momentous year when they so nearly won the title – but did win the Scottish Cup – left Southampton and headed back to Tynecastle, despite offers from two English Premiership clubs to sign him. Graham Rix could scarcely contain his delight at securing the services of the Scotland international. With Rudi Skacel about to serve a suspension, the timing of 'Terry's' homecoming could not have been better timed.

The news of McCann's return was overshadowed by the announcement of the death of former Hearts chairman Wallace Mercer. Mercer was the Romanov of the 1980s, saving Hearts from financial oblivion and overseeing the rise of the Jambos from First Division also-rans to a team regularly challenging for honours and playing in European competition. At the age of just fifty-nine, he had been taken away at a relatively young age but the memory of Wallace Mercer and what he did for Hearts will never be forgotten by those who follow the boys in maroon.

Although saddened by the news of Mercer's passing, Hearts headed for Rugby Park and the clash with Kilmarnock in high spirits. The venue was where this astonishing season had begun in earnest and there were high hopes that the blistering start made by the team back in the summer could be repeated.

Hearts: *Gordon, Neilson, Berra, Webster, Fyssas,*
Mikoliunas, Brellier, Hartley, McCann,
Elliot and Pospisil

Given the team selection for much of this season thus far, there was an unfamiliar look to the Hearts team. Captain Steven Pressley began a two-match suspension and youngster Christophe Berra who had had a smattering of first-team experience in the preceding twelve months took his place. Also missing was the icon of this astonishing season, Rudi Skacel, who was serving a one-game suspension. The surreal nature of the afternoon was completed by not only seeing a Hearts team without the Czech hero but seeing a member of Hearts' 1998 Scottish Cup winning team, Neil McCann, take his place. Terry received a rapturous reception from the three thousand travelling Hearts fans during the warm up and we hoped he could reproduce some of the magic of eight years ago. But the game was to prove a nightmare for McCann and his new team's hopes of landing the league title.

Kilmarnock had shown they were prepared to use the more physical side to their game during the recent Scottish Cup defeat at Tynecastle and so it was that they rolled up their sleeves again on their home patch. After a minute's impeccably observed silence in memory of Wallace Mercer, Killie immediately kicked off on the offensive with Garry Hay firing in a fierce effort that flew just over Craig Gordon's crossbar. To a great cheer from the Hearts support, Neil McCann showed he still possessed the skill for which he was renowned when he set up Calum Elliot with a deft pass but the youngster couldn't control the ball.

It was, however, largely huff and puff for the opening half hour with neither team looking like they were intent on playing silky, stylish football. In truth, Killie looked the better of two distinctly average teams and any hopes the Hearts legions had that McCann might inspire his new teammates to greater things disappeared after just twenty-three minutes when home defender David Lilley lunged in on the Scotland player with a tackle that was almost as late as a number three bus to Gorgie. McCann fell to the ground in a crumpled heap and was replaced by Jamie McAllister. The injury he sustained would keep McCann out for several weeks.

Hearts seemed unsettled by this and Killie proceeded to dominate the rest of the half. Graham Rix must have been happy to get his players in to the dressing room at the interval with the game still goalless. Not for the first time this season, the anonymous Mikoliunas would not appear for the restart, being replaced by Barasa. Whatever choice words Rix may have used at half-time, they had little impact as Kilmarnock took less than a minute of the second half to score. Colin Nish's effort was deflected inside a Hearts penalty box that looked like the Haymarket at rush hour and fell for the unlikely named Danny Invincible who fired past an irate Craig Gordon to put the home side ahead.

And that, my Hearts-supporting friends, was about that. The rest of the game followed the familiar pattern when Hearts have lost this season – missed chances, refereeing decisions that defied logic and increasing frustration. Calum Elliot was having one of those afternoons when nothing went right and his missed effort from six yards after an hour summed up Hearts' day. The JTs never looked like scoring and, but for an astonishing miss from Colin Nish right at the end of the game, they could have lost the game by a bigger margin.

Given that Hearts were without Pressley and Skacel as a result of indiscipline, it was a source of further frustration to see another four Hearts players booked – Julien Brellier in particular was now edging his way to another ban. And, with Celtic defeating Motherwell the following afternoon, Hearts' championship hopes were not so much fading as disappearing altogether. The gap was now ten points. More worrying for the disconsolate Jambos as they headed back to the capital city was the fact that Hibernian and Rangers both won and the gap between second and third place in the SPL was now down to six points. Rangers, at one point fourteen points behind the Maroons, were now, menacingly, just seven points behind. And Hearts' next league game? The little matter of an Edinburgh derby at Tynecastle.

Neil McCann's injury was a bitter blow for Hearts and, while Rudi Skacel would be free from suspension to face Edinburgh's lesser team, the oft repeated claim that Hearts' squad wasn't big enough to challenge for the title was trotted out by the media again.

Hearts: *Gordon, Neilson, Webster, Berra, Fyssas, Mikoliunas, Hartley, Brellier, Skacel, Johnson and Elliot*

New recruit from Yeovil Town, Lee Johnson, made his home debut which, given the enormity of the game, was somewhat surprising. But it soon became apparent why Johnson was given the Edinburgh derby in which to make his first starting appearance in maroon and white – Graham Rix had opted for a 4–5–1 formation with young Calum Elliot operating as the sole striker. We experts in the stands weren't slow in voicing our opinions. Yes, Hearts were without Eddie Jankauskas and Roman Bednar because of injury and Steven Pressley because of suspension and, yes, Michal Pospisil wasn't fit enough to start the game and was on the substitutes' bench – but this was the wee team we were playing and one up front at Tynecastle simply wasn't on. Were Hearts happy to settle for a point? The answer was to become abundantly clear.

Hearts had announced that, as a tribute to Wallace Mercer, there would be one minute's applause immediately before kick-off as a mark of respect. Clearly, given who the opposition were, a minute's silence was never going to work. How unfortunate, then, that the Hibs players and officials chose to ignore the applause and stood motionless whilst the Hearts players and fans and referee Mike McCurry and his assistants loudly applauded the memory of a man who would forever be part of Hearts' folklore.

The game kicked off as usual, with Hearts foraging into the Hibs half and it must have taken Tony Mowbray's men a full two minutes to cross the halfway line. But they did and, with Hearts packing the midfield and hoping to hit their city rivals on the break, it was the visitors who looked the more threatening. Garry O'Connor was given far too much time and space to power in a header which Craig Gordon did well to save. Two minutes later and the Scotland goalkeeper saved equally well from O'Connor's strike partner Derek Riordan as our unease began to grow.

I'm having difficulty finding the keys on my laptop to type these words but . . . Hibs looked the more likely team to score. It seemed only a matter of time before there was a goal – and one duly arrived on the twenty-seven-minute mark . . . at, dear readers, the opposite end from where most of the danger had been thus far. The impressive Takis Fyssas played a pass of some quality to Rudi Skacel who raced to the byline and his deft flick to Paul Hartley was stabbed pass Hibs keeper Brown to put the home team a goal ahead. It might have been against the run of play but few of the dancing Hearts fans in three quarters of the ground cared less.

With six minutes to half-time, Calum Elliot had a golden opportunity to double Hearts' lead when former Hearts colleague Michael Stewart, now in the green and white of Hibs, gave the ball away and Elliot had the seemingly simple job of shooting past Brown and into the net. The youngster did shoot past Brown – but also past the post. It was head-in-hands time for the player and for 14,000 Jambos and, at this point, I wondered if Hearts would regret that miss.

I got my answer four minutes later. A free kick from Paul Hartley was helped on by Christophe Berra, deputising for the suspended skipper, to the ever-alert Rudi Skacel. The Czech midfielder duly despatched the ball beyond Brown and Hearts were two goals ahead. Cue more celebrations from the home support.

Hibernian's hopes of a fightback were destroyed in two minutes before half-time. Having scored his sixteenth goal of the season, 'Ruuuudi' was immediately after number seventeen and burst into the Hibs penalty box where Celtic-bound Gary Caldwell brought the midfield man down. Paul Hartley blasted the subsequent penalty kick high into the net to make the score 3–0 to Hearts and our joy intensified seconds later when Hibs' Gary Smith elbowed Mikoliunas in full view of the referee who had no option but to show the former Aberdeen player a red card. I can't remember enjoying a half-time break as much before – three goals ahead over Hibs with the visitors down to ten men. Hibs early promise had crumbled and the team had seemingly thrown the metaphorical white towel into the ring.

That figure much respected by Hearts supporters – Derek Riordan – didn't appear for the second half, having been replaced by Fletcher while Mikoliunas's habit of only lasting forty-five minutes continued and he was replaced by Cesnauskis. Within five minutes of the restart, many of the Hibs support decided that Derek Riordan had the right idea and also left, influenced no doubt, by Calum Elliot making amends for his first half aberration by heading past Brown on fifty minutes to put Hearts four goals ahead. We forty-something Hearts fans, who still carried the mental scars of the 7–0 drubbing inflicted by the wee team at Tynecastle in 1973, urged Hearts to go for the kill and add three more goals – after all, there were still forty minutes to go.

If Captain Marvel Steven Pressley had been on the field, Hearts may well have done just that but there appeared to be a 'job-done' mentality and Hearts dropped the pace considerably. The spirited Ivan Sproule inspired his Hibernian colleagues to a fightback of sorts and, when Garry O'Connor pulled a goal back with half an hour to go, we realised that, as Hearts supporters, we just wouldn't get away with lighting up the cigars just yet.

The game petered out thereafter but the celebrations among the home support at the final score of Hearts 4, Hibernian 1 were raucous and satisfying. To make things even better, news came through from Celtic Park that league leaders Celtic had squandered a 3–1 lead with eight minutes to go to allow Dundee United to snatch a 3–3 draw. The gap at the top of the SPL between Celtic and Hearts was now eight points with Rangers moving above Hibs into third place following a win over Inverness Caledonian Thistle. But Rangers remained seven points behind Hearts and our city rivals were now nine points behind their big neighbours.

January had been an astonishing month, a month which typified the incredible season that Hearts were having. I headed off for a short break to Egypt with the satisfaction of seeing Hearts restore normal service in the Edinburgh derby.

Next was the not so small matter of taking on Aberdeen in the Scottish Cup at Tynecastle – where Hearts had never beaten the Dons on Scottish Cup business. And February would be but days' old when the astonishing rollercoaster that was season 2005/06 was about to take another huge dip.

This is how the SPL table stood on 31 January 2006:

31 JANUARY 2006

	P	W	D	L	F	A	Pts
Celtic	24	18	4	2	63	26	58
Hearts	24	15	5	4	49	19	50
Rangers	24	12	7	5	44	28	43
Hibernian	24	13	2	9	41	34	41
Kilmarnock	24	10	7	7	44	39	37

FEBRUARY

The final day of January 2006 was, perhaps, one of the most frantic ever seen at Tynecastle. With the transfer window about to slam firmly shut for another six months, Hearts were keen to add to the number of new signings thus far who included Neil McCann, Lee Johnson and Nerijus Barasa. There was little transfer activity elsewhere in Scotland – Rangers had signed Kilmarnock striker Kris Boyd while Celtic had taken on thirty-six-year-old Dion Dublin – but Hearts, as they had done since the season started, stole the show in spectacular style and new signings arrived in Gorgie in droves.

Chris Hackett, a midfield player who had been attracting attention from Hibernian decided to join Edinburgh's big club. Ludek Straceny, a striker, joined the growing Czech colony at Tynecastle. Bruno Aguiar, another midfield player, signed from Benfica, while two defenders, Slovakian Martin Petras and Portuguese Jose Goncalves arrived, as did a backup goalkeeper for Craig Gordon, Frenchman Rais M'Bohli. Finnish striker Juho Makela arrived boasting a remarkable scoring record for HJK Helsinki – thirty-three goals in forty-one games.

But arguably the most spectacular signing of all was the one that required Hearts to pay out a record transfer fee of £850,000. Bosnian winger Mirsad Beslija arrived after protracted negotiations with Belgian club Racing Genk and his glowing reputation was already cause for excitement among Hearts fans who watched events unfold wide-eyed (and in some cases, legless). Some critics had sniped that Vladimir Romanov had still to show the colour of his money. He had answered his critics big time at the end of January.

Less surprising but perhaps somewhat unpalatable in the eyes of some Hearts fans was the appointment of former Hibernian manager Jim Duffy as assistant coach. Duffy was a close personal friend of Graham Rix so it wasn't exactly a bolt from the blue that the former Dundee manager, who had been sacked from the managerial position at Dens Park earlier in the season, should arrive in Gorgie to help out his good friend.

It was against this backdrop that Aberdeen arrived for Scottish Cup business on Saturday 4 February. The Dons could only cast admiring glances towards Gorgie. Their recent record at Tynecastle was not particularly good. Against that, however, was the curious statistic that Hearts had never beaten the Dons in the Scottish Cup, either at Tynecastle or Pittodrie – their only victory coming at Hampden in the 1996 semi-final when a last-minute Allan Johnston goal gave the Maroons a 2–1 win, following a truly awful game. Another huge crowd of over 17,000 packed into Tynecastle to see if the new-look Hearts could finally break the hoodoo.

Hearts: *Gordon, Neilson, Pressley, Webster, Beslija,
Cesnauskis, Brellier, Johnson, Goncalves,
Elliot and Pospisil*

Graham Rix wasn't keen on making too many changes but the suspension of Paul Hartley and the late call-offs by flu victims Rudi Skacel and Takis Fyssas forced his hand. Mirsad Beslija was the obvious choice to replace Hartley while Jose Goncalves replaced Fyssas. Captain Marvel was back from suspension and Michal Pospsil was fit enough to start the game.

Aberdeen brought their usual large travelling support and it was they who were the happier in the early stages as an unusual Hearts line-up struggled to find a level of cohesion. Diamond and Foster had early chances to net Aberdeen's first goal at Tynecastle since Moses was a child but the opportunities weren't taken. Hearts eventually found their feet and a burst of pace from Beslija created a chance for Cesnauskis but the Lithuanian was tracked well by Diamond. After former Jambo Scott Severin and Jamie Smith both tried long-range efforts, one thought back seven days to when Hearts also started sluggishly against Hibernian but still won handsomely. And it was to be a case of déjà vu.

After twenty minutes, Beslija's pass found Calum Elliot who set up Michal Pospisil. The Czech striker chested the ball superbly before striking a fantastic effort from just inside the Aberdeen penalty box past a startled Langfield in the Aberdeen goal. Pospisil ran to the Hearts fans in delight and, while it may have been undeserving on Aberdeen, it was a sublime goal which settled the home side. Fifteen minutes later, after Hearts had at last played some of the football we all knew they were capable of, Cesnauskis crossed for Elliot to slot the ball home for Hearts' second and a place in the quarter-finals of the cup was looking good.

Andy Webster then fouled the visitors' Stevie Crawford who, a year ago, had turned down the chance to move to Tynecastle. Referee Kenny Clark, however, gave no foul and for once Hearts got the rub of the green with refereeing decisions. Aberdeen were furious and their rage deepened on the stroke of half-time when Pospisil was clean through on goal only to be brought down by Diamond. The Aberdeen defender was shown a straight red card (the fifth of his young career) and Jimmy Calderwood's fury turned to apoplexy when referee Clark awarded a penalty to Hearts even though it looked like the offence had been committed outside the penalty box. In the absence of Paul Hartley captain Pressley took the kick and, as against the wee team seven days before, Hearts were 3–0 up against ten men as the half-time whistle blew. And, as against Hibernian, Hearts considered the job done and there were no second half goals to please the baying home support.

Juho Makela did make an appearance when he replaced Calum Elliot but that was about it for the second half action as Aberdeen sought damage limitation while Hearts were content with a place in the quarter-finals of the Scottish Cup. When the draw was made on Saturday evening, Hearts were given another home draw. Their opponents would be Thistle – although whether it would be Inverness Caledonian or Partick depended on the result of a replay at Firhill.

As a Hearts supporter of nearly forty years' standing, I'm a naturally pessimistic kind of fella but even I was encouraged by the fact that this year ends in a six. Hearts won the Scottish Cup in 1896 (even if it was a victory over a minor team), 1906 and 1956. We've been to the final in 1976, 1986 and 1996. True, in these last three years mentioned, Hearts had been well and truly gubbed. But Celtic's demise to a little club in the previous round was matched by Rangers' shock defeat at Ibrox to another little club in round four when Hibernian produced a quite stunning 3–0 win. With both halves of the Old Firm now out of the competition, those of us who like to look at any kind of omen if it will help preserve our sanity were already looking towards 13 May at Hampden Park. But, as a Hearts fan, it doesn't pay to look too far ahead as the next few days proved.

Three days after Hearts' impressive win over Aberdeen, a story broke that alleged that Graham Rix was no longer in charge of team selection. Those bastions of broadcasting, the BBC, stated they had information from two players (they didn't care to name them) that indicated that Vladimir Romanov was now picking the team. It was the story some elements of the press had been waiting for for weeks and Hearts were, once again, hitting the national news headlines. The other story that broke was that Andy Webster had refused the offer of a new contract.

The two stories were immediately linked when it was confirmed that Webster would be on the substitutes' bench for the trip to Dundee United that evening. Alongside him would be Robbie Neilson. Webster and Neilson had been stalwarts of the best defence in the league this season so their roles as substitutes at Tannadice merely added fuel to an already raging fire that the Russian businessman was dictating who would play. Once again the rumour mill was working double time. Fans were quick to assume that Andy Webster's omission from the team could only mean one thing – it was the former Arbroath player who had given the press the story about team selection. Was Romanov furious at Webster's decision not to sign a new deal? A deal, which, the story goes, would have made Webster one of the highest paid players in the club's history. If so, one could understand the Russian telling Graham Rix that he only wanted players in the team who believed they had a future at Tynecastle.

Whatever the rights and wrongs of the story, the dark clouds had returned to Tynecastle once more. But that didn't stop another huge travelling Hearts support heading to Dundee for a game that, if Hearts won it, would take them to within five points of Celtic.

Hearts: *Gordon, Petras, Pressley, Berra, Fyssas, Hartley, Brellier, Skacel, Elliot, Pospisil and Straceny*

Not too many eyebrows had been raised when Hearts had made five changes to the team at the weekend but all hell let loose now that six changes had been made at Tannadice. Webster and Neilson were indeed on the bench – but lost in the furore was the fact that Fyssas and Skacel were back. Petras and Straceny made their debuts and Berra replaced Webster. Beslija and Goncalves had failed to recover from their respective injuries picked up at the weekend.

As against Hibernian and Aberdeen, Hearts made a sluggish start. Much had been made of Hearts making a blistering start to games but running out of energy towards the end of ninety minutes. I wondered if Graham Rix had now instilled a more cautious start in order to preserve energy. Dundee United, now under the managership of Craig Brewster, had already shown huge signs of improvement by coming back from 3–1 down to grab a draw at Celtic Park so it was not surprising to see the Arabs have the better of the first half.

That said, it was Hearts who created the first real chance when debutant Straceny showed an impressive turn of speed down the right wing and fired in an equally impressive cross towards Michal Pospisil. The Czech seemed certain to score but failed to make any contact with the ball and the chance to settle his nervy team had gone. Inevitably, Hearts paid the price when, ten minutes before half-time, United went in front. Mulgrew's cross seemed to confuse Craig Gordon and his uncertainty allowed Grant Brebner the chance to head home. The fact that Brebner used to play for a certain team in Leith wasn't lost on the goalscorer or the hordes of travelling fans.

Mulgrew and Samuel – who had tormented Hearts whilst a Falkirk player two years previously – were causing the Maroons lots of problems and the make-up of Hearts' defence wasn't really helping matters. Captain Pressley had spoken of the need for continuity in team selection, no matter how large the squad, and the Hearts back four were playing like they were strangers – maybe because two of them were.

Hearts started the second half a bit more like their old selves and Rudi Skacel fired in a cross that Calum Elliot headed over – but at least it was a chance and the Maroon Army roared their encouragement. The game was, however, a poor one and it looked like Hearts' not-quite impressive away form was going to continue – a thought that was reinforced when Samuel should have doubled United's lead after fifty-five minutes but he shot over the crossbar from five yards out. Thankfully.

What that did was to rouse Hearts once more and the introduction of Robbie Neilson to a huge approving roar form the Hearts support told its own story. Shortly afterwards, Pospisil, who had been a big disappointment that evening, was replaced by Cesnauskis. With just eight minutes to go, Hearts were awarded a penalty when Robson fouled Steven Pressley. Paul Hartley did his usual no-nonsense job with the penalty and Hearts had rescued a point with a 1–1 draw. They might even have taken all three had Julien Brellier not stupidly got himself sent off in the final few minutes – behaviour which incurred the wrath of his manager after the game.

Given United's resurgence, a point was not a bad result but, when league-leaders Celtic defeated Falkirk the following evening, the gap at the top of the SPL was back to ten points.

It had been another traumatic week for Hearts fans. The morning after the United game, Steven Pressley spoke on behalf of the players and said they were looking for a meeting with Vladimir Romanov to clarify a few matters – matters that undoubtedly included the issue of who was picking the team. An anxious wait ensued for the emotionally battered Hearts fans. Would there be no end to the twists and turns of this incredible season?

The sometimes repetitive nature of Scottish football was clearly illustrated when Hearts next opponents in the SPL were Aberdeen – making their second visit to Tynecastle in seven days. Because Hearts had bolstered their squad with several new players and given the fact they had hammered the Dons in the Scottish Cup, the bookies weren't slow in making Hearts red-hot favourites to win the game, with Jimmy Calderwood's side quoted at 6/1 to record a rare victory in Gorgie. It had been seven years since that had happened and, indeed, more than eleven hours since Aberdeen had even scored a goal at Tynecastle. So you know how the script goes when everyone expects a comfortable Hearts win . . .

Hearts: *Gordon, Neilson, Pressley, Webster, Fyssas, Petras, Hartley, Beslija, Skacel, Elliot and Aguiar*

Now here's a word you probably won't find in the more refined books about Scottish football – dreich. The spell-check system on my PC immediately puts a squiggly red line underneath it but I can think of no better word to describe the afternoon – the weather was damp, windy and miserable and the football on offer equally so. With the controversy over the team selection for the Dundee United game still raging, it was interesting to note that Andy Webster and Robbie Neilson were back in their usual starting places. Losing such an influential figure as Julien Brellier, thanks to his red card at Tannadice, was a blow but Portuguese Bruno Aguiar took his place while record-signing Mirsad Beslija came back into the team.

The customary blistering start Hearts had made to so many games this season was in evidence again as the Maroons swarmed around the Aberdeen goal in the opening stages. Good linking play between Skacel and Fyssas gave the Czech player an early opportunity but his effort flew across Aberdeen's six-yard box when one would have expected Hearts' leading goalscorer to add to his sixteen-goal tally for the season thus far.

On nine minutes, however, Hearts did indeed open the scoring when Skacel left the Aberdeen defence for dead before delivering a low cross into the penalty box and Calum Elliot duly flicked the ball past Langfield. It was the early goal Hearts and the fans had been looking for and, given the previous week's events, we settled back and waited for the onslaught.

With Rangers and Celtic playing each other the next day, Hearts knew that three points against the Dons were a must and we anticipated Hearts going for the kill. Sadly, it didn't happen. Skacel almost set up Elliot again moments later but the midfield player seemed to have too much time to think about what to do and the chance was lost.

What happened in the game thereafter was something of a mystery. It may have been the effects of another traumatic week behind the scenes at Tynecastle. It may have been that, having soundly beaten Aberdeen a week earlier, the players thought they merely had to go through the motions to record another win. Whatever it was, Hearts took their feet off the gas and Aberdeen, slowly but surely, began to take command of the game.

Chris Clark swung in a dangerous cross, which, with wind assistance, dipped in front of Craig Gordon and smacked off the crossbar. Then, a Nicholson free kick was parried by the Scotland goalkeeper as the Dons sensed they could grab an equaliser before half-time. Jamie Smith then had an effort that Gordon did well to tip over the crossbar. Shortly afterwards, Lovell should have restored parity when he scooped Gordon's deflected save from Griffin's free kick past the post from three yards out. With Hearts seemingly ceasing to operate as an attacking force, we spluttered into our half-time Bovril hoping that Graham Rix would be having a few stern words with his players as their 1–0 half-time lead looked perilous.

Unusually, Hearts made two changes for the beginning of the second half but, given their performance for much of the first, this wasn't really a surprise. What was surprising was the substitution of Bruno Aguiar who had, in my view, been Hearts' best player in that opening period. But the Portuguese player had picked up an injury and was replaced by another of Hearts' new signings, Ludek Straceny. The anonymous Martin Petras also made way for Lee Wallace, a welcome sight in this writer's opinion as young Lee is an outstanding talent.

But the second half began in the same manner as the first had ended with Aberdeen on the offensive. Diamond, determined to last for the full ninety minutes this week, had a low shot saved by Gordon. It appeared only a matter of time before Aberdeen got the equaliser their play merited and it duly arrived after sixty-seven minutes. After the normally reliable Hearts defence did a fair impression of the Keystone Cops, the ball broke to former

Hearts favourite Scott Severin. Sevvy's effort on goal blasted off the unfortunate Steven Pressley and spun behind Craig Gordon for the equaliser that had been on the cards for some time.

Frustratingly for the home support, such a setback did not seem to inspire the Maroons to greater efforts for a winning goal and it was Aberdeen who sensed blood and went for the victory. With just three minutes left, Dons substitute Snoyl foxed both Fyssas and Wallace on the right wing before he laid the ball off to Clark whose shot at goal trundled past a startled Craig Gordon for a well-deserved winner for the visitors.

The unusual sound of boos greeted the home players when referee Ian Brines' final whistle blew and the chance to gain ground on Celtic had been lost. Disappointment hung over Tynecastle like the dark clouds which had hung over the place all day as the realisation materialised that perhaps the league championship dream was over – a thought that was to be confirmed when Celtic duly defeated Rangers the day after to open a surely unassailable thirteen-point lead over Graham Rix's side. It was extremely small consolation that, in drawing nothing each at Falkirk, Hibernian had gained just a point on Edinburgh's big club while Rangers stayed eight points behind following their inability to take anything from the Old Firm derby.

The ramifications of another dramatic week was that Hearts' title hopes were irreparably damaged and the battle now would be to try to hang on to second place and the prospect of Champions League football next season. Hearts remained favourites for the Scottish Cup but Vladimir Romanov's dream of seeing Hearts crowned champions of Scotland at the end of his first full season at the club was surely now in tatters.

After the defeat by Aberdeen, the 'who picks the team' row which had erupted the previous week appeared to have been settled. The players requested a meeting with Romanov to 'seek clarification' of the situation and, to this end, Steven Pressley officially met the owner to discuss the matter. The briefest of statements on the official club website shortly afterwards declared that peace had broken out at Tynecastle and everything in the garden was, once again, rosy. Many fans, however, were less than convinced.

And nothing was done to allay their suspicions when another major Monday night news story came from Gorgie. It was announced that Jim Duffy had been appointed Hearts' Director of Football until the end of the season – yes, that is indeed the same Jim Duffy who had been announced as Assistant Coach only a few days earlier. If there were some fans who found this difficult to accept – a sacked Hibernian manager now in charge of football matters at Edinburgh's big club – there were many more who simply didn't understand the appointment. Rix had been Duffy's boss for less than a fortnight and, now, if we were to understand their roles correctly, Rix would be reporting to Duffy. The way this season had been going, the Martians could have landed in Edinburgh's McLeod Street and it wouldn't have created any bigger headlines than those that had been emanating from Tynecastle for the past nine months.

Given Hearts' away record for much of the season, they could at least look forward to their next league game being at Tynecastle – even if it was the visit of bogey team Motherwell.

Hearts: *Gordon, Neilson, Pressley, Webster,*
Fyssas, Cesnauskis, Aguiar, Brellier, Skacel,
Jankauskas and Elliot,

Being Hearts supporters and therefore natural-born worriers, the absence of Paul Hartley due to suspension was a major concern as we supped our pre-match pints. Deividas Cesnauskis was entrusted with the responsibility of deputising for the Scotland internationalist while notable absentees from the great January sales were Martin Petras and Mirsad Beslija who had both struggled to make an impact since their arrival. Graham Rix deemed the pair needed to improve their fitness levels and so it was a more familiar Hearts team that took to the field against a Motherwell side who had become the proverbial pain in the rear for the JTs in recent years. There was a welcome return for Eddie Jankauskas who started the game while his long-term absentee striking partner Roman Bednar was on the substitutes' bench. The duo had been badly missed as Hearts had fallen away in the title race.

What was also familiar was the whirlwind start made by the home team although the opening goal almost came at the wrong end for once. Motherwell striker Richie Foran delivered a cross which seemed harmless enough but the Hearts defence simply looked at each other and allowed Scott McDonald to head the ball against the post before it bounced off the legs of a bemused Craig

Gordon. Captain Pressley scrambled the ball clear and his clearance fell to Takis Fyssas. The bold Greek found Rudi Skacel who bore down on the Motherwell goal before firing in a typical ferocious effort. 'Well keeper Meldrum could only parry the effort and there was Eddie Jankauskas to blast the rebound high into the net to mark his return by putting Hearts ahead. Ten minutes later, the lead was doubled.

Elliot and Cesnauskis did well on the right wing before the ball broke to Jankauskas twenty-five yards out. With a confidence that hadn't always been in evidence this season, the former FC Porto striker struck a quite superb shot which almost burst the Motherwell net to give Hearts a 2–0 lead. Eddie took the acclaim of the rapturous home support and we looked forward to another convincing Hearts win – except, of course, this is Hearts.

More good play from Eddie J. almost let his compatriot Cesnauskis in but his effort was blocked. As Motherwell sensed they might be on the end of a doing, Terry Butcher's men resorted to all-too frequent physical challenges that appeared to unsettle the home team. Kerr and former Jambo Jim Hamilton were booked as the game occasionally threatened to get out of hand. 'Hammy' and McDonald both came close to getting the visitors back in the game but half-time arrived with the Maroons two goals ahead. Referee Charlie Richmond had given some bizarre decisions in that first half and he was given a 'special' reception from fans of both sides as he headed up the tunnel with his hapless assistants at the break.

As in recent weeks, Hearts seemed slow to come out of the traps at the start of the second half and Motherwell looked the team likelier to score after the restart. Jim Hamilton thought he had done just that but his effort was ruled out after goalie Craig Gordon had been fouled in the build-up. Sensing the tide had turned somewhat, Graham Rix decided to replace the tiring Eddie Jankauskas with another striker who was returning from lengthy absence – Roman Bednar. Eddie J. was given a standing ovation as he left the field and the fans remained on their feet to greet the Czech striker who had not played for the first team since before Christmas. His influence was there for all to witness and Hearts regained the impetus.

With Motherwell's efforts looking like they were going to count for nothing – despite their sometimes over-physical approach to the game which did little to enhance their reputation as one of the best young sides in Scotland – Hearts duly sealed all three points when Calum Elliot latched on to a cool lob from Skacel to deliver a fine lob of his own over Meldrum to end the scoring at Hearts 3, Motherwell 0. Given the problems The Steelmen had caused Hearts over the previous couple of years, this was a welcome and important win for Graham Rix's side.

The SPL title may have gone but second place in the league still meant the potential of Champions League football next season. In Glasgow, Rangers had finally managed to beat Hibernian and so Hearts' lead in second place was now seven points, although the Ibrox side were now looking like the form side among the main contenders for the runners-up spot in the league.

There would, however, be an interlude in the battle for this as Hearts resumed Scottish Cup business the following week with the visit of Thistle to Tynecastle – not

Inverness Caledonian Thistle as most of us had believed but Second Division Partick Thistle who had knocked the Highlanders out of the cup after a penalty shoot-out in the Firhill replay. With Hearts uncomfortably installed as evens favourites to lift the trophy – odds I had never seen in my life before – the Maryhill Jags would head to Edinburgh with nothing to lose. As the cliché goes – this was their cup final.

Hearts: *Gordon, Neilson, Pressley, Webster,*
Fyssas, Cesnauskis, Brellier, Hartley,
Skacel, Jankauskas and Elliot

Being a cup game, Paul Hartley took his usual place in the middle of the park as his suspension was for league games only. Bruno Aguiar was the unlucky player to make way for the Scotland player and, given the frenzied trans-fer activity in Gorgie of a month earlier, it was interesting to note that not one of the eleven players who had arrived at Tynecastle during the transfer window was starting against Thistle.

Another 16,000-plus crowd turned up despite the insistence of Sky Television that the game kick off at 12.15 on a Saturday lunchtime. Plenty of time afterwards then to help in the search for a new kitchen was the suggestion put forward by the infamous Mrs Smith but I countered this by saying that, as this was a cup tie, there may well be extra time and penalty kicks. I omitted to tell her that this normally only happens in the replay but I knew that, to her mind, this would be a technicality.

Partick Thistle brought a sizeable support, as we knew

they would, and Hearts made a decent start, as we hoped they would, despite the fact that Thistle clearly hoped for a psychological advantage by winning the toss and forcing Hearts to play towards the Gorgie Road end in the first half – something which rarely happens and hadn't happened so far in the season. But only five minutes would elapse before Hearts put a spoke in the wheel of that particular argument.

Paul Hartley delivered a fine cross from the left to the head of Eddie Jankauskas who flicked a header past Thistle keeper Arthur to put the home side one goal ahead. We sat back and waited for the goal rush – after all, Thistle were Second Division opponents and, as another old cliché goes, they wouldn't have wanted to lose an early goal. Right? Well, if you're a Hearts fan, you should know the script by now . . .

The rest of the match was a painful affair. Rather worryingly, in this writer's eyes, Hearts seemed to have developed a penchant for scoring early and then sitting back thinking the job had been done. Thistle came more and more into the game and Craig Gordon was being called into action more often than was comfortable. McConalogue and Roberts were proving to be a handful for the home defence and the restlessness among the home support became palpable. The only Hearts player to be making an impact was the oft-maligned Deividas Cesnauskis but he didn't seem to be getting the support required from the likes of the unusually quiet Rudi Skacel and unusually anonymous Julien Brellier.

Half-time arrived with a few boos from the maroon-clad support despite their team having a one-goal lead. It appeared it wasn't only the Hearts fans who were unhappy – Graham Rix sent his players out early from their half-time break to do warm up exercises on the corner of the pitch – a sight I can't remember seeing before in nearly forty years of following this damn team of ours.

Sadly, such a ruse didn't appear to have much effect as the second half began the way the first half ended – with the Glasgow Jags on top. On the hour mark, came an astonishing moment. Thistle were awarded a free kick on the edge of the Hearts penalty box. Billy Gibson let rip with a powerful effort that deflected off Jankauskas, wrong-footed Craig Gordon and seemed to be flying into the net for a deserved equaliser. But the Scotland goalkeeper twisted his huge frame at the last moment to palm the ball away for a corner and Hearts breathed again. It was a quite stupendous save from the best goalkeeper in the country. And moments later Thistle would be made to suffer again.

Cesnauskis collected the ball on the right-hand side of the field. The Lithuanian danced his way to the edge of the Thistle penalty box before curling a magnificent shot high into the net to rather unfairly double Hearts' lead. The home support heaved a huge collective sigh of relief – but, being Hearts fans, the relief was never going to last long.

With twelve minutes left, substitute Roman Bednar was through on goal with a chance to settle the tie. The Czech striker rounded keeper Arthur and there seemed to be minimal contact with the Thistle custodian. Bednar went down, rather theatrically it has to be said, and this was enough for referee Thompson to flash the striker a yellow card. As Bednar had already been booked for the heinous crime of kicking the ball away, this was his second yellow card and so Hearts would play out the final twelve minutes with ten men.

The Thistle fans sensed the tide was turning. Moments later their perceptions were proved correct when Mark Roberts, almost at walking pace, ghosted past a static Hearts defence and placed a fine shot past Craig Gordon to put Thistle back in the game. With their lead now slender and the team now numerically disadvantaged, panic seemed to sweep through the home players and support. Graham Rix sensed this and replaced Cesnauskis with young defender Christophe Berra. A couple of minutes after scoring, Thistle should have equalised when more abject defending from the home team allowed Darren Brady time and space in the penalty box but, thankfully for those in maroon, his shot from ten yards out blazed high into the Gorgie Stand. Eventually, the final whistle blew and the Hearts fans could scarcely have felt so much relief. Hearts' poorest display of the season had seen them outplayed by a Second Division team at home and they could thank their lucky stars they were in the draw for the semi-finals.

It was a draw that included Hibernian who had no such problems in defeating fellow Premier League side Falkirk. Also in the hat were Second Division Gretna who had defeated First Division St. Mirren and two other First Division sides – Hamilton Academicals and Dundee who had drawn their quarter-final at New Douglas Park and would replay at Dens Park. Hearts and Hibs were the only SPL teams left and the inevitable happened when the semi-final draw was made forty-eight hours later.

Hearts would play Hibernian the day following April
Fools' Day. For football supporters in Edinburgh it would
be no laughing matter – for the winners would surely have
one hand on the famous old trophy?

This is how the SPL table stood on 28 February 2006:

28 FEBRUARY 2006

	P	W	D	L	F	A	Pts
Celtic	27	21	4	2	74	28	67
Hearts	27	16	6	5	54	22	54
Rangers	27	13	7	7	46	31	46
Hibernian	27	14	3	10	48	36	45
Kilmarnock	27	12	8	7	52	43	44

MARCH

'The talk o' the toon are the boys in maroon' goes part of the lyrics of one of Scottish football's most famous anthems but the talk o' the toon at the beginning of March was the Scottish Cup semi-final draw which had paired Hearts with Hibernian. And the hot topic of debate was where the game would be played. The Hearts fans, players and management wanted the game to go ahead at the obvious, sensible choice – Murrayfield Stadium in Scotland's capital city. Hibernian fans weren't so sure while Easter Road boss Tony Mowbray wasn't convinced the playing surface at the home of Scottish rugby would be suitable for such an important game. But the prospect of fifty thousand rival fans heading along the M8 on a Sunday lunchtime – yes, folks, those nice people at Sky TV wanted the game to kick off at 12.15 on Sunday 2 April – didn't appeal to the better nature of the Chief Constable of Strathclyde Police. The grey suits at Hampden considered the views of both clubs (although not the views of those people without whom there would be no game at all – the supporters) before deciding the game would be played at Hampden anyway – another win for the bureaucrats . . .

As Hearts began the month of March, the semi-final was still a month away and the furthest thing from the mind of Graham Rix as he took his troops to Livingston for another vital league game. The game was the preferred choice of Setanta Sports that weekend and so was moved to Sunday – by which time Rangers and Hibernian had both increased the pressure somewhat by winning against Falkirk and Dundee United respectively.

Paul Hartley and Julien Brellier were suspended for this game and skipper Steven Pressley had failed to recover from the virus that had forced him to miss Scotland's friendly international defeat by Switzerland the previous midweek. On top of all that, Livingston were playing their first home game under their new head coach – a little fella still revered in Gorgie . . . a certain John Robertson who, a year earlier, had been manager of Hearts. So, if the Livi Lions weren't hungry for victory before, then Wee Robbo would certainly instill a desire in his new charges. It was a huge challenge for Graham Rix's side.

Hearts: *Gordon, Neilson, Berra, Webster, Fyssas, Cesnauskis, Petras, Aguiar, Skacel, Jankauskas and Elliot*

Back in September, this same fixture attracted over 8,000 fans – 6,000 of them Jambos – and Hearts, then under George Burley, cruised to a 4–1 victory. Now, six months later, the official attendance was 5,058 and not even the Hearts support had bought their full allocation of tickets. With Christophe Berra and Martin Petras being given the chance to show what they could do, it was a somewhat unfamiliar Hearts starting line-up.

Andy Webster was made captain for the day in the absence of the missing Captain Marvel and this was a fair turnaround in affairs from four weeks previously when Webster was dropped from the first team. But 'Smokey' led the team out with pride with his one-year-old son Christian in his arms. The little lad left the field in tears and the Hearts support almost joined him in the crying stakes when Livingston almost took a disturbingly early lead after a totally unmarked Greg Strong blazed a header over the bar when he really should have scored.

Hearts looked sluggish in the early stages and Livi's on-loan Hibee Sam Morrow was causing problems for the Hearts defence – something that keeper Craig Gordon was clearly unimpressed by as he spent much of those early minutes berating those in front of him. So it was something of a surprise when Hearts went in front after seventeen minutes.

The ball ping-ponged off several players on the edge of the Livi penalty area before breaking to Bruno Aguiar whose deflected shot spun over the head of the despairing Roddy McKenzie – another ex-Jambo with more than a point to prove – to give Hearts a lead they scarcely deserved.

This seemed to settle the visitors although Livi still looked threatening going forward with young Dorrand tormenting the Hearts defence. At the other end, Aguiar and Skacel both came close to doubling Hearts' lead before Calum Elliot was unceremoniously upended on the edge of the penalty area. The Hearts support shouted for a penalty kick but it looked outside the box and therefore a free kick would have been in order. But, inexplicably, referee John Underhill ignored the claims, waved play on and the home team breathed a huge sigh of relief – as they did again moments later when Martin Petras gave us a glimpse of what he's capable of when he drove in a ferocious twenty-yard effort which McKenzie did well to palm over the crossbar.

Half-time arrived with the visitors in front. However, the second half began in much the same fashion as the first with the home team in the ascendancy. Five minutes in and Hearts gave away a needless free kick on the left. Richard Brittain delivered a teasing cross – one that teased the Hearts defence so much that they all left it to each other and the ball sailed into the net beyond Craig Gordon to give the home side the equaliser they deserved. The absence of a certain Mr Pressley was never felt so acutely – and, moments later, it could have been worse.

Another sweeping move by Livi – belying their bottom of the table status – saw youngster Allan Walker all on his own just six yards out. He seemed certain to score until Craig Gordon once again underlined his worth to Hearts with a fantastic block to keep Hearts on level terms. As the Livingston players held their heads in their hands the inevitable happened when Hearts, very much under the cosh, went ahead again with eighteen minutes left. A quite magnificent pass from Robbie Neilson found Cesnauskis down the right touchline. The Lithuanian winger delivered a fine cross to his countryman Eddie Jankauskas who flashed a header past McKenzie to put Hearts 2–1 ahead.

Big Eddie had been anonymous for much of the game but his goal was an important one – although this didn't stop Graham Rix replacing him with Roman Bednar shortly afterwards. Eddie's final action was to set up Rudi Skacel who was clean through on goal with only McKenzie to beat. But Rudi had been off colour the whole afternoon and tried to round the keeper instead of flicking the ball over him and surely securing a Hearts victory. McKenzie took the ball off him and the chance was gone, as was Rudi himself when Chris Hackett, making his Hearts debut, replaced him.

We all wondered how much we would regret Rudi's miss when Livingston equalised in spectacular fashion with thirteen minutes left. Yet more sloppy defending from the maroons saw the ball break to the former Dundee player with the famous name on the edge of the penalty box. Without breaking his stride, Dave Mackay unleashed an unstoppable shot into the roof of the net and Almondvale erupted once more. Two goals each and yet again Hearts fans pondered another two points dropped on the road.

Livi were on top again now and there was the distinct possibility that Wee Robbo's team would deprive the visitors of anything at all – a thought given some credence when Martin Petras volleyed over the crossbar from just five yards out. But with just three minutes remaining, Roman Bednar took advantage of a slip from Jason Dair, raced into the penalty box and dispatched the ball beyond the grasp of keeper McKenzie to make it Livingston 2, Hearts 3. The final whistle sounded soon after and the travelling support roared with relief more than anything else. It had been a close call but Hearts maintained their eight-point lead over Rangers and nine over Hibernian.

They had less than a week before they considered another tough away fixture – at Inverness Caledonian Thistle.

Hearts: *Gordon, Neilson, Webster, Berra, Fyssas, Hackett, Hartley, Aguiar, Cesnauskis, Bednar and Elliot*

If Hearts fans were concerned by the absence of some key players at Livingston, their anxieties increased considerably when they saw the team line-up in the Highland capital. Julien Brellier continued his suspension but Steven Pressley was still missing as a result of a virus that was causing more than a little concern. Rudi Skacel's ankle injury didn't recover in time for the match and Eddie Jankauskas also failed to attain full fitness, something that had blighted the Lithuanian since his move to Tynecastle – a move which happened in considerably warmer climes than was evident at the Caledonian Stadium.

Mid March it may have been but the weather that greeted Hearts and Inverness Caledonian Thistle would not have been out of place in Siberia. Portuguese Bruno Aguiar wore a pair of gloves and who knows what under his shirt. The good news was that Paul Hartley returned after sitting out the Livi game and Skacel's rare absence meant a first-team start for Chris Hackett.

To describe the conditions as windy is akin to saying Vladimir Romanov likes the odd bit of attention now and again and the gale played a part in the opening chance when Craig Dargo got on the end of his goalkeeper's clearance (the ball was heading for the Moray Firth before the wind blew it back into play) and tested Craig Gordon.

At the other end, Roman Bednar, making his first start since being injured in September, was causing a problem or two for the home defence for whom Darren Dods was given the customary reminder from the visiting support that he used to play for a lesser team. Chris Hackett was also prominent and his pace was a feature of a reasonable opening spell from Hearts despite neither goalkeeper being seriously troubled. On the half-hour mark, Cesnauskis eagerly intercepted a loose pass from the home side and made a beeline to Mark Brown's goal. Chesny then elected to pass to Bednar but the Czech striker's effort was straight at the goalkeeper and a decent chance to open the scoring had gone. Caley Thistle then pressed as the first half drew to a close and Gordon saved well from Hart.

A couple of weeks earlier, Graham Rix demonstrated what he thought of Hearts' shoddy first-half performance against Partick Thistle by sending the players out on the pitch at half-time to perform warm-up exercises. Lo and behold, the Hearts players were out again during the interval at Inverness but I suspect this was more to do with adapting to the bitterly cold conditions rather than any comment on Hearts' first-half display which was passable but not brilliant.

Caley Thistle had the wind to their advantage as the second half got underway and Berra and Webster certainly weren't short of anything to do. Jamie McAllister – who, somewhat surprisingly, given his lack of appearances in a maroon jersey of late, had been named in the Scotland Future squad to face Turkey at Inverness the following Wednesday – replaced the tiring Hackett with twenty-five minutes to go. But it was the home side who were coping better with the conditions and Bayne came worryingly close to giving the home side the lead. Having said that, a looping ball in the Caley Thistle penalty box caused consternation among the home defenders with Bednar about to pounce before the home side cleared their lines.

Thus the game petered out, the only other incident of note being when the luckless substitute, Jamie McAllister, had to be replaced by Jose Goncalves after sustaining an injury. Perhaps Jamie didn't fancy returning to ice station Inverness with the Scotland Future squad four days later! (Only kidding, Jamie, if you're reading this.)

The game ended goalless and so another two points were dropped on Hearts' travels. It has to be said that Inverness Caledonian Thistle had proved very tough opponents and not only in this game but also throughout the season. In three games against the Highlanders, Hearts had scored just one goal and recorded just one win – and that was a fortuitous victory during the Burley era in September.

With Rangers closing the gap to six points, following their inevitable victory over Kilmarnock at Ibrox, the pressure was back on Hearts in the race for second place. And that pressure would reach fever pitch the following week when their main rivals for that second spot would be visiting Tynecastle. A year after the infamous 'Andy Davis' incident, Hearts v. Rangers 2006 promised to be another cracker!

Hearts: *Gordon, Neilson, Pressley, Webster, Fyssas,
Cesnauskis, Brellier, Hartley, Skacel,
Jankauskas and Bednar*

With Hearts' injuries clearing up and players back from
suspension it was heartening to see Steven Pressley returning to his customary role in the back four. Julien Brellier
returned from suspension and Rudi Skacel and Eddie
Jankauskas also returned from injury. Eddie J. partnered
Roman Bednar up front which meant Calum Elliot had to
be content with a place on the substitutes' bench. With the
atmosphere red hot – Hearts fans were occupying a section
of Tynecastle usually reserved for visiting Old Firm supporters after controversially reducing Rangers ticket allocation – Rangers knew this was a game they could not afford
to lose. A nine-point gap between the two sides would surely prove insurmountable and the Ibrox men signalled their
early intention when Chris Burke surged into attack.

But it was Hearts who went ahead in just the ninth
minute after turning defence into attack in devastating
fashion. Cesnauskis won a fifty-fifty ball and lobbed a fine
pass to Paul Hartley. The Scotland player showed that he
is one of the quickest players in the game by racing down
the wing before looking up to see Eddie Jankauskas in the
penalty box. Hartley's cut back was met by the Lithuanian
hit man who drove the ball into the net to give Hearts an
early lead. Tynecastle erupted into a cacophony of noise
and Eddie was soon smothered by his delirious teammates.

Rangers responded as we all knew they would and
Thomas Buffel had an excellent chance to level the
score but Craig Gordon saved his weak effort. The Hearts

goalkeeper was called into action again soon afterwards when Peter Lovenkrands was given far too much time on the ball which enabled him to fire in a low shot that Gordon tipped round the post. It was another warning that Rangers were determined they weren't going to lose this match.

For some curious reason, Hearts sat back and seemed content to let Rangers come at them – always a dangerous ploy and especially so against either of the Old Firm. Hearts fans urged their team to get forward but the midfield seemed strangely anonymous, with the big long punt up the park seemingly the preferred option. This cautious approach only served to create hesitancy in the home defence and a mistake by Robbie Neilson let Barry Ferguson in but, thankfully for Robbie, his teammates scrambled the ball clear.

Frustration in the home ranks was growing, particularly at the sight of young Rangers full back Alan Hutton fancying his chances of scoring with a rasping effort from thirty yards out which flew over the crossbar. Up to this stage, Rudi Skacel had scarcely figured in the game – his normal attempts to rouse the home support not withstanding. But, as half-time approached, the Czech player showed dogged determination to resist the challenge of two Rangers players before playing a fine pass to the ever-busy Cesnauskis. The Lithuanian delivered a fine cross into the Rangers penalty box but visiting keeper Waterreus managed to get to the ball before Roman Bednar which was just as well for Alex McLeish's side or it would have been 2–0 to the home team.

That said, the game should have been all square at the break when, on the stroke of half-time, Rangers' Chris

Burke showed fine skill to evade several, albeit lukewarm, tackles from the Hearts defence before sending over a fine cross. Thomas Buffel only had to tap the ball into the empty net but the unfortunate Belgian completely missed the ball, leaving his young Scots teammate gazing to the sky in exasperation.

Half-time ended with the home side one goal to the good and there was a special reception for referee Craig Thomson and his assistants as they left the field. Some of the officials' decisions for both teams in that first half simply defied logic. And there was no change after the restart. The second half was merely minutes old when Rangers' pony-tailed Croatian striker Dado Prso deemed fit to deliver a forearm smash into the head of Steven Pressley. Thomson wasted no time in reaching to his pocket and we waited for the red card to be shown. But the colour was yellow and Hearts protestations fell, as usual, on deaf ears.

Frustration mounted among the home players and supporters as one baffling decision followed another from the referee. But ten minutes into the second half, Hearts had yet another cause to appreciate the outstanding talent of their young international goalkeeper. To celebrate the award of their 10,000th free-kick that afternoon, Lovenkrands fired in a shot that was deflected towards Buffel. The Belgian took the ball on the volley from ten yards out and we waited to see the net bulge for a fine Rangers equaliser. The Rangers fans had already began to cheer the goal when Craig Gordon leapt to his right and tipped the ball past the post. It was yet another astonishing save from the Hearts number one and his relieved team mates rushed to offer their gratitude as disbelieving Rangers players prepared to take the resultant corner kick.

Sadly Hearts didn't hold out for too much longer. Rangers substitute Kris Boyd, signed from Kilmarnock during the January transfer window, passed to Prso who in turn, passed to Burke. The young Rangers winger fired in an effort that fell kindly to Buffel whose shot cannoned off Gordon before nestling in the net. Cue big celebrations from the visitors and gasps of exasperation from the home support. Hearts had rarely threatened Rangers goal since going ahead and if containment was their plan it clearly had not worked. As against Celtic on New Year's Day, Hearts had handed the initiative to the visitors and Rangers sensed blood.

They were certainly winning the physical battle and, when Prso swung another elbow which caught Robbie Neilson, we looked for, if not a straight red card, the second yellow which would have spelt the end of the game for the Croatian striker. Can you guess what happened, dear reader? Mr Thomson awarded Hearts a free-kick and waved Prso away. Perhaps I'm doing Craig Thomson a disservice here – there may have been a FIFA directive that declared elbow challenges legal and, if so, I apologise to the official for casting doubt on his judgement . . .

When Prso blatantly fouled Julien Brellier shortly afterwards, the referee still refused to take further action. However Gers boss Alex McLeish did and promptly replaced Prso before the red card followed the red mist. Graham Rix meantime made a change of his own when he replaced the largely ineffectual Roman Bednar with young Calum Elliot who could have considered himself very unfortunate not to have started the game.

With the clock ticking fast, Hearts seemed to have at last woken up to the fact that they could still win the game and extend their points advantage over Rangers to nine points. Cesnauskis was causing panic in the Rangers defence but it was the unlikely figure of Robbie Neilson who so nearly proved to be the match winner. Those of us who were in Basle towards the end of 2004 couldn't quite believe our eyes when young Robbie drove home the winner in the UEFA Cup tie against the Swiss champions. Once more, Neilson ambled forward with the Rangers defence seemingly believing he was not a threat. The Scotland Future player unleashed a ferocious shot from twenty-five yards which rattled both the crossbar and the Rangers goalkeeper. The final whistle sounded soon after and it seemed a strange anticlimax for a game that had promised so much.

Rangers had come to Gorgie intent on three points and were doubtless disappointed they headed back to Govan with only one. Hearts, on the other hand, had spurned the chance to extend their lead in second place in the SPL to nine points but would still be relatively content that the gap remained at six points.

The previous day, Hibernian had conceded a last-minute goal at Motherwell – and, with it, two points – as they were held to a 2–2 draw. The wee team had now slipped to fifth place in the SPL, one point behind Kilmarnock who, under Jim Jefferies, continued to defy the odds.

For Hearts, there would now be three crucial games away from Tynecastle, which could perhaps shape the remainder of their season. At the beginning of April, they would face Hibernian in the much awaited Scottish Cup semi-final at Hampden before heading back to Glasgow on league business three days later to face champions-elect Celtic.

These were two huge games that would test the resolve of this Hearts team but, before all that, there was the trip to the new Falkirk Stadium, a venue where Hearts had spilt their first league points of the season back in October. And where they would face a Falkirk side fighting for SPL survival. We hoped Graham Rix would be able to go one better than his predecessor and record a Hearts win at Falkirk. But, three days before the game, it was bombshell time at Tynecastle once again . . .

On the morning of Wednesday 22 March 2006, Hearts announced that Graham Rix's contract with the club had been terminated with immediate effect. Chairman Roman Romanov said, in an official statement that appeared on the club website:

We have been disappointed with the performance of the team. Results were not what they should have been. We also felt that some of the signings made in January were not appropriate for Hearts. In addition, the events, which occurred in February when Hearts played Dundee United, including the way in which some information reached the public domain, were disappointing to us. I'd like to thank Graham Rix for all his hard work at Hearts. He gave 100% but ultimately it did not work out. Vladimir Romanov and the club's management felt that something had to be done quickly. We owed it to the fans.

The 'Turmoil at Tynecastle' headlines were splashed all over the papers again. Eleven days before the most important Edinburgh derby game in one hundred and ten years – the Scottish Cup semi-final at Hampden – Hearts had dismissed their third head coach in less than a year. It was, as ever, captain Steven Pressley who spoke on behalf of the players and he told the throng of waiting journalists at Hearts' academy at Riccarton that the players were devastated. In the interim period, Lithuanian Valdas Ivanauskas was appointed first team coach until the end of the season, assisted by the ever-present John McGlynn who must have started to wonder why he had to go through all this again. The value of McGlynn throughout a sometimes-tortuous year for the Hearts players cannot be overestimated.

The reaction of many Hearts supporters seemed to be one of surprise rather than shock. After the events surrounding George Burley, Phil Anderton and George Foulkes and the alleged team selection by Vladimir Romanov at Dundee United, we knew to expect the unexpected. It's fair to say that many fans thought Rix would have left Tynecastle at the end of the season in any case. For it to happen at a crucial time in the season seemed to be yet another bizarre twist to a plot that Agatha Christie would have been proud of.

Two things puzzled this writer. One was the assertion by Roman Romanov that some of the players brought in during the January transfer window weren't of the standard expected at Hearts. No names were mentioned but it didn't take rocket science to figure out that Neil McCann, Lee Johnson and Chris Hackett were those players. Secondly, newly appointed Director of Football

Jim Duffy was also shown the door at the same time as Graham Rix. No immediate reason was given for this and, as the former Dundee manager had only been in post for four weeks, it's difficult to work out what he had done wrong. Whatever the reasons, this latest bombshell from the Romanovs did little to display Hearts in a shining light and the fans were once again unhappy. True, many weren't happy at the appointments of Rix and Duffy in the first place but the timing of their departure had caused upheaval once again at a time when this was the last thing the club needed.

Vladimir Romanov continued his flirtation with controversy even in the hours that followed Rix's departure. His declaration that he wanted Rix out several weeks before did nothing to dispel the feeling that the Russian millionaire was one of the most ruthless men in the game, a reputation forged with FC Kaunas.

Meanwhile, the rumour mill was in overdrive again. The *Edinburgh Evening News* stated that one-time Rangers, Liverpool and Scotland midfielder Graeme Souness – whose uncle played for Hearts in the 1950s – had been contacted about coming to Tynecastle. Such a scenario was enough to make your eyes water – Souness had always had a hard-man reputation, both as a player and manager and one winced at the prospect of 'Chop Suey' as the tabloids like to call him locking horns with Vlad the Impaler. Surely a marriage made in hell? Souness denied the claims soon after.

Nevio Scala publicly declared his interest in the Hearts job. The former Parma coach had been linked with the job back in the summer but it was believed he needed more time to learn the Scottish culture and language

(Scotland being the only country in the world where two positives are joined to form a negative – do you fancy the Hearts job? 'Aye, right!') The quaint Scots phrase that the hard working Graham Rix had learned towards the end of March was 'Yer tea's oot'.

Valdas Ivanauskas was now charged with leading the shell-shocked Hearts players along the home straight of this astonishing season. Ivanauskas knew Vladimir Romanov better than most – he had already worked for him at FC Kaunas – so perhaps had a better insight into how Vlad's mind worked.

Falkirk beckoned in the last Saturday in March. We all wondered what kind of team would play and what mental state would they be in?

Hearts: *Gordon, Neilson, Pressley, Goncalves,*
Fyssas, Cesnauskis, Brellier, Hartley,
Skacel, Jankauskas and Bednar

One of the many controversies to afflict Hearts this season came in February when preparations for the trip to Dundee United were knocked for six with the news that Andy Webster had been dropped from the team, allegedly under Vladimir Romanov's instructions, after 'Smokey' refused to sign a new contract. Seven weeks on and with Graham Rix now no longer at the club, Webster was missing again from the Hearts team to face Falkirk. In fact, the former Arbroath centre half was nowhere to be seen in Falkirk and the official explanation given was that he was suffering from a virus and was sent home. His replacement at the New Falkirk Stadium was Jose

Goncalves. Other than that it was the same team that drew with Rangers although there was the welcome sight of Sammy Camazzola on the substitutes' bench for the first time since before Christmas.

The cynics who suggested that Romanov had picked the team for this important game may well have been confused by the sight of Julien Brellier taking up his usual place in midfield. If VR was picking the team it wouldn't have been a wild assumption that the Frenchman would have joined Andy Webster on the sidelines given the numerous press reports that Romanov didn't rate the player. But, then again, anything was possible this season.

There was another large and vocal travelling support as the game got underway and their fervour was stoked further by the host DJ electing to play the Hibernian anthem, The Proclaimers' 'Sunshine on Leith' as the teams took to the field. It certainly seemed to have an effect on the players as Hearts started in typical fashion, camped in the Falkirk half. Five minutes in and Rudi Skacel had the first real attempt on goal when he drove in a shot that the Falkirk keeper Howard did well to keep out.

Hearts were dominant but still the goal would not come and, after quarter of an hour, skipper Steven Pressley was forced into action as the home side took a corner. The captain took what looked like a severe blow to the head and, not for the first time in a Hearts shirt, the Scotland player spilt blood and had to leave the field for treatment. Down temporarily to ten men, Hearts almost went behind when Craig headed a Rodrigues cross wide of goal when it seemed easier to score.

We anxiously waited for the Hearts captain to return

and he did soon after – and as he did Hearts went in front. Skacel took off on a typical mazy run that drew many of the Falkirk team towards him. His accurate cross was met by Paul Hartley who despatched the ball into the net to put Hearts one goal ahead and spark celebratory scenes in the away end. Hearts should have doubled their lead soon after when Gordon's clearance was knocked on by Roman Bednar sporting a Mohican hair cut. The ball fell to Eddie Jankauskas but Big Eddie's effort was blocked. Eddie had another chance moments later but he seemed to misjudge the pace of Cesnauskis's cross and another chance went begging.

Falkirk were still very much in the game as their counter-attacks proved and, just as we thought we would get to half-time with our lead intact, the Bairns were awarded a penalty kick after referee Freeland adjudged there was hand ball in the Hearts box. Alan Gow's penalty kick was saved by Gordon but the former Airdrie United player buried the rebound and so the teams trooped off at half-time on level terms.

Concern for Steven Pressley grew when the captain failed to reappear after the break, his replacement being Christophe Berra. With Hearts needing to win the game and having seen their slender lead vanish, those more pessimistic Hearts fans (me included) worried about what would happen given that two rocks of the Hearts defence – Webster and now Pressley – were both missing. And it clearly inspired Falkirk who took the game more to Hearts than they had done in the first half.

And The Bairns defied their nickname by upping the

physical ante. Julien Brellier went down after appearing to have been hit by Dodd but no action was taken against the Falkirk player. Rudi Skacel had been deemed by the home team and supporters to be going to ground too easily and the home players appeared to have targeted the Czech international with some crunching tackles. Twenty minutes into the second half, Acting Head Coach Ivanauskas decided to take Skacel off for his own safety and he replaced him with Calum Elliot. The Hearts fans warmly greeted the move as their team was now playing with three players up front – something which seldom happened under Graham Rix. It was an obvious indication that Hearts knew they had to win the game. But the move almost backfired when Lesincel set off on a lung-bursting run for the home team before thankfully running out of steam as he shot at goal.

If that was a worrying sight, so too was the spectacle of Hearts' defensive rock shattering again as Robbie Neilson appeared to suffer a similar fate to his captain when he rose for a high ball. Robbie left the field to be replaced by Martin Petras for the final ten minutes and it looked like Hearts would have to hold on for a draw.

But, oh, ye of little faith! With nine minutes to go, Calum Elliot sprinted forward in a breakaway Hearts move. The youngster laid the ball into the path of Jankauskas whose effort on goal wasn't the cleanest shot ever struck but had enough power to spin past Howard and give the Jambos a crucial lead. Hearts hung on to record a vital away win and retain their six-point lead over Rangers as the chase for second place in the SPL and that coveted Champions League spot entered the home straight.

Rangers inevitably had defeated Dunfermline Athletic at Ibrox (although it took another late winner from them to clinch the points). That was expected but we all cheered the news from Easter Road. Inverness Caledonian Thistle had defeated Hibernian for the third time this season meaning there was now a thirteen-point gap in the league between the Edinburgh rivals. With Kilmarnock throwing away a two-goal lead and dropping two points at Tannadice it was now clearly a two-horse race for Champions League football next season. And, for the wee team, the defeat was not the best preparation in the world for the next game up – at Hampden in eight days.

That was a source of small comfort for Hearts supporters at the end of yet another dramatic month. But we cheered further when Craig Gordon put an end to media speculation by signing an extension to his contract which had been due to end in 2007. The best goalkeeper in Scotland had committed himself to Hearts until 2009. Not only that but he backed Vladimir Romanov to deliver success for Hearts in that time. It was much needed good news for Hearts fans – as another incredible month ended, we needed all the inspiration we could get . . .

This was how the SPL table looked at the end of March 2006:

31 MARCH 2006

	P	W	D	L	F	A	Pts
Celtic	31	25	4	2	83	30	79
Hearts	31	18	8	5	60	26	62
Rangers	31	16	8	7	54	33	56
Kilmarnock	31	14	9	8	57	50	51
Hibernian	31	15	4	12	43	43	49

APRIL

As April began, both Hearts and Hibs were the talk of the whole country as the biggest Edinburgh derby in over a century – the Scottish Cup semi-final at Hampden Park – took place on Sunday 2 April 2006. The build-up was intense, the anticipation mind-blowing and the mood of supporters of both teams was fraught. The game had been on my mind since the draw had been made several weeks earlier and now the moment had arrived. Defeat to Hibernian is a bitter experience at the best of times – thankfully this doesn't happen too often. Losing a cup semi-final is a bitter experience at the best of times – sadly, this does happen all-too frequently for Hearts fans. Many people said that losing a cup semi-final to Hibernian just didn't bear thinking about – but the problem was that it did bear thinking about. The difficulty was how to cope with such a scenario. And so it was on a dull Sunday morning that the mass exodus from Edinburgh headed to Scotland's largest city, nerves frayed, for a game that would ensure bragging rights in the capital city for years to come.

Hearts: *Gordon, Neilson, Pressley, Webster, Goncalves, Cesnauskis, Hartley, Aguiar, Skacel, Jankauskas and Elliot*

There had been jibes from some Hibs fans that they would have the larger of the supports as all tickets for the green and white end had been sold while, apparently, Hearts had not sold all their briefs. But, as the game kicked off at a gloomy, cold Hampden, the truth was there for all to see. While there was a smattering of empty seats in the Hearts end, there were huge gaps at the other side of the stadium. Row after row of empty blue seats gave the obvious statement that Hibs had come nowhere close to selling all of their ticket allocation. Although the game was live on Sky Television – there was another ridiculous kick-off time of 12.15 p.m. on a Sunday to accommodate this – the absence of a strong Hibs support was, nevertheless, something of an embarrassment for those associated with the Easter Road club. If they could-n't sell tickets for a Scottish Cup semi-final with their Edinburgh rivals . . . well, need I say more? And those of the green-and-white persuasion wondered why Hearts fans referred to them as the wee team?

Much had been made of Hibernian having several key players missing – Derek Riordan was suspended while Scott Brown was also out – but Hearts too were without the suspended Roman Bednar and, perhaps more impor-tantly, Julien Brellier. The Frenchman had been a key part of Hearts' season and his absence would be sorely felt. Acting Head Coach Valdas Ivanauskas brought back Calum Elliot and gave Brellier's role to Bruno Aguiar.

Interestingly, the former Kaunas coach opted for Jose Goncalves at full back, opining that the Portuguese player's pace would be better at handling the speedy threat of Hibs' Ivan Sproule.

Semi-finals are not renowned for their free-flowing football but this game began in promising fashion when, in the opening minute, Rudi Skacel – who had taken more than his fair share of flak during the week for his 'diving' antics at Falkirk a week earlier – raced past Whittaker and delivered a fine cross into the Hibs penalty box. Jankauskas's attempt to get on the end of this cross was thwarted by a combined effort from Hogg and Caldwell. Then, minutes later Eddie J. had a chance of his own but his effort was too direct at Hibs keeper Malkowksi and the wee team breathed again.

Tony Mowbray's side came close themselves with long-range efforts from Fletcher and Whittaker, the latter of which forced Craig Gordon to tip over the crossbar and we heaved a sigh of relief as we did again shortly after when Caldwell headed past with the Hearts defence looking less-than assured.

The game was more entertaining than we had expected it to be given that the stakes were so high but, from our vantage point in the West Stand, we were enduring the game rather than enjoying it and many Hearts fans cursed the newly introduced smoking ban in enclosed public spaces in Scotland. Couldn't the Scottish Executive have waited a couple of weeks?

Paul Hartley was the Hearts player causing his former teammates most grief and the Hibs keeper brilliantly turned his free-kick over the bar. But, on twenty-five minutes, Hearts went ahead with a goal that was typical of the team this season. Hibs were on the attack when Benjelloun lost the ball on the edge of the Hearts penalty area. Hartley collected the ball and raced down the middle of the park before passing to Jankauskas on the left. Eddie ran on to the edge of the Hibs penalty box before passing back to Hartley who, with the outside of his foot, slipped the ball past Malkowksi to give Hearts the lead. Cue rapturous celebrations among the huge Hearts contingent. It was a marvellous goal even if it was slightly against the run of play and it gave the Maroons the confidence to take control of the game.

Hibs were resorting to long-range efforts although Robbie Neilson made a brilliant tackle on Sproule as the first half came to its conclusion. But, no sooner had the fourth official indicated there would only be one minute's stoppage time at the end of the first half, than Steven Pressley suffered a head knock and, while he returned to the field after lengthy treatment, it was obvious he would be in no fit state to continue after the break. Ivanauskas made the obvious switch for the start of the second half by replacing the captain with Takis Fyssas. Goncalves switched to centre half and the Greek international occupied his familiar fullback berth.

Being a goal down, it was expected that Hibs would start the second half on the offensive and they did with Kevin Thomson having an early chance. We fidgeted nervously in our seats constantly looking at the time elapsed on the giant Hampden scoreboards as Hibs continued to exert pressure. Hearts fans urged their side to score a second goal and Paul Hartley duly obliged with an hour of the game gone. Fyssas had ambled forward to the edge of the Hibs penalty box where he was rather needlessly upended. Cue Hartley who assessed the options available to him in the box where Eddie J. and Calum Elliot among others were lurking.

But Hartley proved, not for the first time, that he has brilliant vision. Spotting that Malkowski had inexplicably left a gap at his near post, the Scotland star delivered a brilliant cross that went straight into the net past the bemused Hibs goalkeeper – 2–0 to Hearts and we danced on the steep slopes of the old stadium!

We knew Hibs would storm forward looking for the goal that would bring them back into the game and the ever-dangerous Steven Whittaker fired in an effort which produced a brilliant save from Craig Gordon. But, as Hearts sensed victory, our emotions were tempered some-what with the sight of Jose Goncalves in a crumpled heap just behind Gordon's goal. The goalkeeper had obvious concern for his teammate but was deemed to be time wasting by referee Stuart Dougal who booked Scotland's number-one number one. Goncalves required several min-utes' treatment and the worrying sign of a neck brace being used emphasised that the Hearts keeper had been right to be worried.

Goncalves eventually left the field (thankfully it turned out to be nothing more serious than concussion) and Hearts had to do another patchwork job on their defence. Mikoliunas came on which meant Rudi Skacel was deployed at fullback and we hoped this disruption would-n't give Hibs the green light to get back into the game. We needn't have worried.

Mikoliunas showed his determination by superbly taking the ball off Sproule. The Northern Ireland international's response was to haul the Lithuanian down before inexplicably standing on his back. As this was in full view of Stuart Dougal, the referee had no choice but to send Sproule for an early bath – much to the delight of the Hearts support. Shortly afterwards, Hibs further contributed to their own downfall when a pass back to Malkowksi was casually anticipated by the Hibs goalkeeper who let Eddie Jankauskas nip the ball from his toes, go round him and slot the ball into the empty net. 3–0 to Hearts and the game was over! With just nine minutes to go, we knew that not even Hearts could throw this away and a place in the Scottish Cup Final was ours – a fact that thousands of Hibs fans acknowledged by heading for the exits.

However, there was still time for one more Hearts goal. Substitute Michal Pospisil raced through on goal only to be pulled back by Hibs' Gary Smith. As happened in the last Edinburgh derby at Tynecastle, the former Aberdeen player was red-carded for denying a goal-scoring opportunity. The resultant penalty was expertly converted by Paul Hartley to complete the former Hibee's hat-trick against his old club and his delight at this achievement was there for all to see.

The final whistle sounded soon afterwards and Hearts fans and players celebrated a famous 4–0 victory and a place in the Scottish Cup Final. The biggest Edinburgh derby in over a century had been a comprehensive victory for the biggest club in Edinburgh – and how we celebrated as we headed back to Auld Reekie. The Tynecastle

Arms rocked that Sunday evening as we savoured the third time we had put four goals past the wee team this season – and a Scottish Cup Final in which our opponents would be, astonishingly, Second Division Gretna who had defeated Dundee in the other semi-final at Hampden the day before. While the nation would undoubtedly be rooting for the underdogs – the first time a team from the third tier of Scottish football had reached a cup final – Hearts would be overwhelming favourites to win the trophy they had last captured eight years previously. It was a brilliant weekend – and it had been the Edinburgh derby to beat all other Edinburgh derbies (including a certain result in 1973).

After the celebrations had started to recede, there was the small matter of Hearts' next league game just three days later – a trip to Celtic Park. Having led the league by five points at one stage this season, Hearts now knew that a win for Gordon Strachan's men would see them clinch the championship in front of their own supporters. And, with Rangers now just three points behind Hearts (they had defeated Dundee United a couple of hours after Hearts' Hampden triumph), Hearts knew the importance of taking something from the east end of Glasgow.

Hearts: *Gordon, Neilson, Webster, Berra, Fyssas, Mikoliunas, Brellier, Hartley, Cesnauskis, Bednar and Jankauskas*

With central defenders Steven Pressley and Jose Goncalves both missing after suffering concussion during the demolition of Hibernian, young Christophe Berra was recalled to the team that would be out to spoil Celtic's championship party. There was also a surprise start for Saulius Mikoliunas in place of Rudi Skacel who had to be content with a place on the substitutes' bench. Roman Bednar replaced Calum Elliot in attack while Julien Brellier was back from suspension.

The usual frenzied atmosphere at Celtic Park was intensified by the importance of the occasion. Hearts started brightly but the old cliché of trying to keep things tight for the first twenty minutes was blown to pieces after just four minutes. A long clearance from Celtic keeper Boruc bounced somewhat fortuitously for John Hartson who fired in a shot from the edge of the Hearts penalty area which bounced and spun beyond the outstretched fingertips of Craig Gordon to give the Hoops the early lead they craved. This prompted a cacophony of noise from the cauldron that is Celtic Park and Hartson and Zurawski went close to extending the champions elect's lead shortly after. That said, Hearts weren't totally out of things and Roman Bednar forced Boruc into a fine save as the Maroons signalled their intentions that they weren't there merely as a supporting act. Bednar then collected a free kick from the new Hammer of the Hibs, Paul Hartley, which the home defence cleared for a corner and one sensed slight unease emanating from the home support.

After Mikoliunas threatened down the wing, hopes rose among the eight-hundred strong visiting support that Hearts could grab an equaliser before half-time although Zurawski almost doubled Celtic's lead after being set up by Hartson. Thank heaven for Andy Webster! The only other effort of note in a strangely subdued first half was a half-hearted attempt at goal from Cesnauskis but Chesny's effort posed more of a threat to the Celtic ball boys standing trackside than to the home goal. As referee Dougie MacDonald blew for half-time, the home side were ahead by a single goal. Hearts had played reasonably well and had plenty of possession but, despite all the pre-match talk, appeared to lack the belief that they could actually win the game.

Valdas Ivanauskas may well have held similar thoughts as Hearts came out at the start of the second half looking more determined to spoil the party. Hopes rose when Christophe Berra caused panic in the home defence allowing Andy Webster to stab the ball into the net but it was clear the 'goal' was scored from an offside position and Celtic breathed again. Michal Pospisil then replaced Eddie Jankauskas and the Czech striker didn't take long to make an impact, firing in a shot that Boruc saved well. With Celtic looking nervous, it was Hearts who were on top in the early stages of the second half and the home fans' uneasiness increased when Hearts' top goalscorer, Rudi Skacel, replaced Mikoliunas as Hearts sought the equaliser.

Brellier's return to the team following suspension was pivotal but the Frenchman collected his now almost-customary booking when he fouled Maloney before Roman Bednar then appeared to be felled by Bobo Balde in the Celtic penalty box and we looked to the referee for the penalty decision. A penalty against Celtic at Celtic Park in a game which if they won would secure the league title? You can guess the outcome dear readers . . . Nonetheless the decision enraged coach Ivanauskas on the touchline. The former FC Kaunas coach's reaction prompted

Hearts' old adversary, referee Dougie MacDonald, to send him to the stand. So Celtic clung on for the 1–0 win which secured the SPL flag – deservedly so as the twenty-point gap at the top of the SPL told its own story.

Hearts' lead over Rangers in the chase for second place was now just three points with six games remaining. Celtic had secured the championship before the infamous SPL 'split' – the last five games of the season see the top six teams play each other one more time. Dunfermline Athletic were Hearts' last opponents before the split – and Hearts knew they could ill afford to drop any more points.

Hearts: *Gordon, Neilson, Pressley, Goncalves, Fyssas, Mikoliunas, Aguiar, Hartley, Cesnauskis, Bednar and Pospisil*

As I headed for my pre-match pint in the now smoke-free Station Tavern, I got caught in a heavy shower of hail and rain and I hoped the dark clouds overhead weren't a sign of impending gloom for my team. In the end, I needn't have worried. There was a celebratory air about Tynecastle as Hearts marked the occasion of the 120th anniversary of the first game at the ground with a souvenir programme and special cards for fans in the Wheatfield Stand to hold up at kick-off. Hearts had officially opened Tynecastle on 10 April 1886 with a 4–1 win in a friendly over Bolton Wanderers – and, no, I wasn't at the game before you ask!

A century and a score years later, Hearts faced the challenge of Dunfermline Athletic. But, not for the first time this season, Hearts' team selection threw up a surprise or two. Andy Webster, who still had not agreed to sign a new deal to keep him at Tynecastle, was listed as a substitute, as was Julien Brellier. Also due to feature on the substitutes' bench was Rudi Skacel – but Hearts' leading goalscorer was nowhere to be seen. The rumour mill immediately released a statement declaring that the Czech was none too pleased at the acting Head Coach's decision to name him as a substitute and had stormed out of Tynecastle.

The absence of Webster, Brellier and now Skacel merely enhanced the claims that Vladimir Romanov was picking the team, particularly as 'forgotten men' Mirsad Beslija and Juho Makela were sitting alongside Webster and Brellier on the bench. Eddie Jankauskas would surely have made it a trio of Lithuanians in the starting eleven had the former Champions League winner not succumbed to the ankle injury that forced him to come off at Celtic Park in midweek.

Now please excuse me if this is beginning to sound a tad repetitive but Hearts began the game at an astonishing pace and were soon camped in the Dunfermline half. A mere thirty seconds had elapsed when Cesnauskis picked up a loose pass from the visitors and fired in a fierce effort which whistled past the post of Pars keeper Alan McGregor. Chesny's compatriot, Mikoliunas, tried a similar effort seconds later but this time McGregor was forced into an impressive save as the small pocket of Dunfermline fans in the corner of the Roseburn Stand must have begun to fear the worst.

Their fears were confirmed after just seven minutes when a Robbie Neilson throw-in reached Michal Pospisil on the edge of the six-yard box. The visiting defence clearly didn't reckon the Czech striker posed much of a threat as they allowed the Hearts man to tap the ball into the net past a startled McGregor to give the home team a well-deserved early lead. If Dunfermline's usually ebullient manager, Jim Leishman, wasn't too pleased with his team's defending, then he would have been downright furious seven minutes later when Hearts doubled their lead. Neilson skipped down the right wing before delivering a cross to the head of Roman Bednar. The other half of Hearts' Czech strike force rose unchallenged to send a looping header into the net and put Hearts on easy street – with less than fifteen minutes played.

It was all Hearts and they were now playing some delightful football, with crisp passing movements turning the beleaguered Pars inside out. Paul Hartley and Bruno Aguiar were dictating the midfield and some of Hearts' football was a joy to watch – the best they had played in weeks. It was no surprise when Hearts went three up after just twenty-three minutes. Once more, Robbie Neilson was involved, collecting a pass from Hartley before setting up Mikoliunas. The Lithuanian who, a year ago, was serving a five-match ban for his indiscretion with assistant referee Andy Davis, brushed aside the challenge of a Pars defender before firing a shot past McGregor into the corner of the net. A quarter of the game gone and the match was effectively over as a contest.

Takis Fyssas then crossed for Bednar but the striker's effort was blocked by an increasingly desperate Dunfermline defence before Fyssas himself was well wide with an effort which posed a danger only to the large number of

Hearts fans in the Roseburn Stand. Cesnauskis and Hartley came close to putting Hearts out of sight but a highly impressive first half ended with Hearts settling for a 3–0 lead – and a standing ovation from the home support.

Gone were the long-ball tactics favoured by Graham Rix and in their place were some skilful interchanges of passes which left Dunfermline players bemused. Our concerns that Hearts may struggle without key players such as Webster, Brellier and Skacel were unfounded. The team selection was the most blatant sign yet, in my view, that Hearts' Russian owner was influencing team selection. But that first half was enthralling so, if Vlad was picking the team, then it was clearly working!

The second half began with Fyssas displaying a quite sublime piece of skill down the left side of the field. Showing a deftness of touch so sadly lacking in today's game, the Greek internationalist dummied his way past a startled Dunfermline defence before crossing into the penalty box. The ball was scrambled away by the visiting defence but it was a piece of skill that had the home fans on their feet in admiration. Bruno Aguiar was putting in a fine performance in midfield and his effort from twenty yards out gave McGregor another scare. It was, once again, all Hearts although Dunfermline passed up the one genuine chance that came their way when Andy Tod was given a free header from eight yards out, his effort going over the crossbar.

This being Hearts' third game in six days, Valdas Ivanauskas decided to freshen things up with Makela and £850k man Beslija introduced to the fray, replacing goalscorers Pospisil and Mikoliunas respectively. Paul

Hartley left the field soon after to a huge ovation from the home support. His replacement was Julien Brellier. The more cynical among us pondered Ivanauskas's chances of getting the job of Head Coach on a permanent basis as not only had he taken off Vladimir Romanov's favourite son – Mikoliunas – but he had brought on a player allegedly not thought very highly of by the Russian – Julien Brellier.

With nine minutes to go, Hearts added a fourth goal when Juho Makela headed Aguiar's corner home for his first goal for Hearts' first team. The match had been ended as a contest some time before but Aguiar's game ended moments later when he was the victim of an astonishing lunge from Dunfermline's Greg Ross. Referee Charlie Richmond immediately flashed a red card to Ross and Hearts' Portuguese player was unable to continue. The game ended with Hearts 4–0 winners and, with Rangers defeating Motherwell 1–0 at Ibrox, Hearts had maintained their three-point advantage over Alex McLeish's side but increased their goal advantage to thirteen.

With the SPL now split for the final five matches of the season, the SPL chiefs clearly saw the battle for second place and its subsequent Champions League spot as the main event of the closing act of the season. The fixtures were announced immediately at the end of the games on 8 April. Hearts would face, in sequence, Kilmarnock at Tynecastle, Hibernian at Easter Road, Celtic at Tynecastle, Aberdeen at Tynecastle and – the main event of the final five games – Rangers at Ibrox for the final league game of the season. So for the SPL run-in, Hearts would have to travel outside Edinburgh only once – and the more optimistic among the Hearts support hoped that, by the final league game, second place in the SPL would be secure. But, as most of us realists all too readily acknowledged, nothing was ever straightforward with Hearts.

Next up then, was a Kilmarnock side who were still chasing a UEFA Cup place. The sell-out signs were once again posted outside Tynecastle.

Hearts: *Gordon, Neilson, Berra, Goncalves, Fyssas, Mikoliunas, Aguiar, Hartley, Skacel, Jankauskas and Bednar*

There was at last some decent weather to greet another huge crowd at Tynecastle as the battle for second place in the SPL and that all-important Champions League place took an earnest turn. Not for the first time this season there was cause to mull over the Hearts team selection. There was no Andy Webster in the starting line-up – not an earth-shattering surprise given the former Arbroath defender continued to refuse to sign a new contract keeping him at Tynecastle – but Hearts fans looked collectively aghast with the non-appearance of Steven Pressley. However, there was nothing sinister about the skipper's absence – his recurring back problem forced him to sit out this game, meaning Jose Goncalves partnered Christophe Berra in central defence. Rudi Skacel replaced Cesnauskis with Eddie Jankauskas also back in the starting line-up.

The game kicked off with immediate concern for Robbie Neilson who was the victim of a challenge that left the Scotland Future player poleaxed on the turf. The fullback resumed moments later but, if it had been Killie's intention to prevent Hearts from starting the game at their usual frantic pace, then it worked. An unmarked Eddie J. couldn't direct his header towards goal in the opening minutes but it was Jim Jefferies' side who looked more threatening in those early stages. Steven Naismith – newly voted Scotland's Young Player of the Year – headed straight at Craig Gordon when he really should have scored, while Garry Hay went close with a free kick.

The home team, however, spurned the best chance of all. Bruno Aguiar, getting through a power of work in midfield, drove into the Killie penalty area before setting up Jankauskas. Big Eddie's effort was palmed away by keeper Alan Combe but the ball fell to Roman Bednar in front of an open goal. Quite what the big Czech Republic striker was thinking of is unclear but his effort on goal was closer to the corner flag than it was to being on target.

Paul Hartley then went close with a free kick but the apprehension in the air steadily grew as a well-organised Killie defence kept Hearts at bay. The visitors still looked dangerous on the counterattack with former Jambo Allan Johnston pulling the strings in midfield. At this stage seven days earlier, against Dunfermline, Hearts were three goals to the good and cruising to victory but this was an altogether much tighter game and our anxiety increased after half an hour when Jose Goncalves left the pitch injured and was replaced by Ibrahim Tall, a player fast becoming an enigma. He had been at Tynecastle for several months but was only now making his first-team debut.

Rudi Skacel fired in a screamer from twenty-five yards before Hearts thought they had opened the scoring at last when Bednar scrambled the ball past Combe, only for referee Smith to whistle for a foul on the keeper. Shortly afterwards, the Lithuanian connection looked like paying dividends when Eddie J. sprinted into the Killie penalty box and waited for his compatriot Mikoliunas to feed him the perfect cross from the right. But Miko's cross almost had the power of an Exocet missile and the ball ended out of play on the other side of the field.

There were anguished cries from the home support but things could have been much worse when, on the stroke of half-time, young Berra appeared to trip Killie's Danny Invincible on the edge of the Hearts penalty box. I feared not only a free-kick to the visitors in a dangerous position but a red card for the Hearts man as it looked like he had denied Invincible a goalscoring opportunity. But the majority of fans inside Tynecastle breathed a huge sigh of relief as referee Smith waved play on. Killie's assistant manager Billy Brown flew into a fury on the touchline and one could understand why. Half-time arrived with the game goalless and Hearts looking distinctly out of sorts.

Feeling a sense of injustice, Killie began the second half on the offensive with Naismith a constant thorn in the flesh of the home defence. Takis Fyssas, in particular, was having a torrid time and Invincible came close to giving the Ayrshire men the lead. Hearts, though, showed why they are one of the best teams in Scotland with a sweeping move down the left that should have broken the deadlock. Skacel found Jankauskas who ran at the Killie defence before finding Paul Hartley with an exquisite pass. The Scotland star was through on Combe but his lob over the keeper also cleared the crossbar and the home fans' wailing increased, particularly when news broke of Rangers taking the lead against Aberdeen.

But there was relief all round on sixty-eight minutes when Skacel ran at the visiting defence only to be fouled on the edge of the penalty box. Hartley stepped up to take the free kick and his superb delivery from twenty-two yards sailed into the net past a stranded Alan Combe. Hearts' joy was intensified with the news from Ibrox – former Hearts player Scott Severin, had equalised for Aberdeen and the battle for second place had turned once more.

But the game in Edinburgh wasn't over yet. Kilmarnock had a great chance to draw level when Colin Nish met Invincible's cross but he appeared to be distracted by his own teammate and Craig Gordon produced yet another fantastic save to retain Hearts' lead. Substitute Deividas Cesnauskis was making his presence felt with some wonderful and determined play in midfield and, with just four minutes left to play, the Lithuanian danced past the startled Killie defence before shooting for goal. Combe saved his effort but the ball spun in the air for Christophe Berra to head home his first goal for the Hearts first team and three points were secure. Berra had been immense throughout the game and his goal was a fitting reward for an outstanding performance.

The gamed ended at 2–0 to Hearts and Stadium Announcer Scott Wilson confirmed soon after the final whistle that Rangers had dropped two points in a 1–1 draw with Aberdeen – a team the Ibrox side had failed to beat this season. Hearts were now five points clear of Rangers with just four games remaining.

There was further joyous news for Hearts' fans with

the news that Craig Gordon had won the Scottish Football Writers' Player of the Year Award. It was a well-deserved accolade for the Scotland goalkeeper – the first goalkeeper to win the award since Andy Goram in 1993 and the first Hearts player to win it since Sandy Jardine twenty years earlier. Gordon had been in brilliant form all season and Hearts supporters felt privileged to witness such an outstanding talent in a Hearts jersey.

The following weekend looked like proving pivotal in the race for Champions League football. Hearts faced a trip across the capital city to face Edinburgh's second club the following Saturday. They knew that a win there would open up an eight-point gap – at least for twenty-four hours before Rangers faced the emotional wringer that was the Old Firm derby at Celtic Park a day later. Hearts fans licked their lips – the appetising prospect of Champions League football was now hovering into view!

Hearts: *Gordon, Neilson, Tall, Berra, Wallace, Cesnauskis, Hartley, Aguiar, Mikoliunas, Bednar and Elliot*

The second Edinburgh derby in three weeks, now on more familiar territory than the Hampden Hammering of the Hibs in the Scottish Cup, kicked off with the usual impassioned atmosphere with the travelling Hearts legions taunting their city adversaries with a chant indicating that, when Hearts are next at Hampden for the cup final, they will be there. However which Hearts players would be there was alarmingly becoming unclear. Steven Pressley was still injured and yet again there was no Webster or

Skacel. Rudi was at least on the substitutes' bench but Webster was sitting in the stand alongside Jankauskas. The feeling persisted that the Scotland defender had played his last game for Heart of Midlothian. Days later, Vladimir Romanov indicated this would be the case when he said that, as Webster had not put pen to paper on the new contract offered to him – and did nothing to allay the rumours linking him with Rangers – he only wanted players who were committed to Hearts. This angered Tony Higgins of the Players' Union but it's fair to say that the majority of Hearts fans were behind the Russian on this decision.

The game began in typical derby fashion with the ball akin to a hot potato for many players as both teams sought an early breakthrough. Despite the frantic pace there was little sign of a goal until the fourteenth minute. And unfortunately for Hearts it came at the wrong end and stemmed from a mistake by a player who had been quite brilliant for the maroons all season. Paul Hartley looked unsure of his next move as he assessed his options in midfield and was dispossessed by Jay Shields. The diminutive Hibee seized his chance and sent Ivan Sproule down the right wing. Sproule fired in a half-decent cross that landed at the feet of Derek Riordan. Despite Fletcher looking to be in an offside position – standing in front of the Hearts keeper – Riordan took a touch before delivering a fine finish past Craig Gordon from fifteen yards to put the home side a goal up. Cue goading from those in a less privileged position . . .

Riordan had a chance to double Hibs' lead soon after when he ran in on Gordon but Paul Hartley made amends for his earlier error with a quite brilliant tackle before seeing the ball run out of play. As in the derby defeat in Leith in October, Hearts looked strangely out of sorts and it took half an hour before the JTs managed an effort on goal worthy of writing about when Mikoliunas drilled in a volley which was saved by the much-maligned Hibs goalkeeper Malkowski. After Riordan came worryingly close again, we began to think that, if Hearts could just get to half-time only a goal down, we would be doing well. Then, deep into first-half stoppage time, a long forward pass from Robbie Neilson found Roman Bednar. The Czech striker incurred the wrath of the visiting fans with a woeful first touch and Caldwell had the seemingly straightforward task of shepherding the ball back to Malkowski. But the keeper appeared to let the ball slip from his fingers and Bednar followed up to fire the ball into the empty net to level the score.

It did appear to be a turning point in the game as Hearts began the second half as the more dominant team with Bednar, Aguiar and Cesnauskis all firing in shots at goal. The best chance, however, fell to Ibrahim Tall who had a free header just six yards out. The Senegalese defender would never have a better chance to score his first Hearts goal but, inexplicably, he headed wide and the chance was gone. And, inevitably, Hearts paid the price with twelve minutes left. New Hibs boy Benjelloun capitalised, if you'll excuse the pun, on some sloppy defensive play by the visitors to fire in a shot past Craig Gordon to win the game for Hibernian. A second defeat of the season for Hearts at Easter Road so I hope you'll forgive the abbreviated version of events – there's no point in Hearts fans dwelling on losing the Edinburgh derby. Suffice to say that Hearts had won the derby match that really mattered three weeks earlier.

With Rangers securing a goalless draw with Celtic the day after, the gap between Hearts and Rangers was now down to four points. A week earlier, we had been celebrating a five-point gap with the possibility of eight if results went as expected after the Edinburgh and Glasgow derbies. Now the gap was half that and Hearts knew the likelihood was that they would go into their next game the following Sunday just a single point ahead of Rangers who played Kilmarnock on the Saturday. And Hearts' next opponents? Champions Celtic at Tynecastle.

Hearts: *Gordon, Neilson, Pressley, Tall, Fyssas, Cesnauskis, Aguiar, Hartley, Skacel, Jankauskas and Bednar*

By the time of the game against Celtic, Rangers had indeed defeated Kilmarnock. The Ibrox side won 3–1 at Rugby Park, after coming back from a goal down, and so the pressure piled on Hearts once more. There had much talk during the build-up to the game about Hearts using 'alternative treatment' in a bid to help players overcome injuries quicker. There was the usual smirking from those who thought they knew better but the return of Steven Pressley appeared to justify that decision. Takis Fyssas, Rudi Skacel and Eddie Jankauskas also returned to the team and another huge crowd greeted the teams with a tumultuous roar.

Celtic knew all about Hearts' penchant for starting

games at pace and it was the Parkhead side who started on the offensive when Stephen McManus – who had scored twice on the Hoops' last visit to Gorgie – had a great chance to put the champions ahead within three minutes but his close-range effort was superbly blocked by Craig Gordon. If young McManus was frustrated by the heroics of Scotland's number one goalkeeper he was in despair moments later when his next effort on goal flew into the net – the Celtic net. Rudi Skacel was fouled on the left wing and Paul Hartley delivered a telling cross into the Celtic penalty box. Telling because McManus leapt to head the ball past his own keeper to put Hearts one goal ahead.

The home fans duly celebrated and they were in raptures just two minutes later. This time Roman Bednar was brought down on the edge of the penalty box. With Celtic keeper Boruc trying to organise his defensive wall, referee Alan Freeland asked Paul Hartley if he wanted to take a quick free kick. The Scotland star wasted no time in saying yes and duly planted a superb shot past the wall and the stranded Celtic goalkeeper. Hartley was almost smothered by his teammates and the home crowd almost brought the Tynecastle stands down with their delirious appreciation. Hearts were 2–0 up on Celtic with less than ten minutes played. But, hang on – we've been here before. New Year's Day to be precise. And look what happened then.

Back in January, Rudi Skacel passed up a great opportunity to put Hearts three goals ahead by half-time. Almost four months to the day, Skacel again had a great chance after he embarked on a mazy run which had most of the Celtic defence trailing in his wake. The Czech star's effort on goal, however, smacked against the post and the more pessimistic Jambos groaned their shouts of, 'Here we go again!'

Hearts came forward again and a brilliant passing move, which involved the impressive Ibrahim Tall, Takis Fyssas and Eddie J., gave Roman Bednar a chance but Celtic defender Paul Telfer cleared the danger. But this delighted the home support who bellowed their encouragement as Hearts tried desperately to avoid the mistakes of the first day of 2006. It was something of a concern then to see Celtic proceed to dominate the remainder of the first half with Roy Keane and Neil Lennon – something of an unpopular figure at Tynecastle and not because he was wearing gloves on the warmest day of the year so far – both firing in long-range efforts. Keane had also missed an absolute sitter from just six yards out when he scuffed his shot. There was just enough time for Deividas Cesnauskis to hare down the left wing and fire in a brilliant cross that agonisingly fell just beyond Eddie Jankauskas.

Half-time arrived soon after and Hearts remained 2–0 ahead. Were we watching a rerun of the New Year's Day game, which, to all intent and purposes, ended Hearts' title hopes? Or would Hearts hang on for a crucial three points in their quest for a Champions League place? As the teams took to the field for the second half, the legendary Scott Wilson, Stadium Announcer extraordinaire, declared that the Hearts players faced possibly the most important forty-five minutes in the club's history – so, no pressure, then. You could almost hear Steven Pressley thinking, 'Thanks, Scott!'

As expected, it was Celtic who went on the attack and Zurawski blasted in an effort from ten yards that Craig

Gordon did well to parry as the nerves among the home support began to jangle. It was all Celtic at the beginning of the second half and Roy the Bhoy Keane headed just over the bar as the feeling grew that Hearts really needed a third goal.

In the sixty-third minute, the home support's prayers were answered. Cesnauskis cleared the danger from his own penalty area and found Hartley. Showing the vision that has made him one of the best players in Scotland, Paul delivered a quite brilliant pass to Roman Bednar. The Czech striker collected the ball and, despite appeals from the visitors for offside, buried it past Boruc from just inside the penalty area. Hearts 3, Celtic 0 and surely it was now game over!

Want-away Celtic star Stilian Petrov then came on as a substitute and he immediately tested Craig Gordon. But the Scotland keeper was determined to keep a clean sheet. Hearts coach Ivanauskas then made a straight swap, replacing Roman Bednar with Michal Pospisil before making tactical substitutions with Christophe Berra replacing the hard-working Tall and Nerijus Barasa making his home debut by replacing compatriot Cesnauskis. Eddie Jankauskas almost made it 4–0 with a chance near the end before Craig Gordon once again saved brilliantly from Petrov. By this time many of the Celtic fans were heading for the exits – soon after being bizarrely accompanied by the Hearts fans in a chorus of 'Let's All Laugh at Rangers' – and Hearts ended the game worthy 3–0 winners. The home players received yet another standing ovation as Hearts lead over Rangers reverted to four points – with just two games left.

It had been a long time since Hearts had scored three goals without reply against Celtic and we headed out of Tynecastle on a sunny afternoon knowing that 3 May was just three days away. 3 May is synonymous with one of the worst events in Hearts' history – the day they lost the league championship with just eight minutes to go at Dundee's Dens Park, at the end of the 1985/86 season. Twenty years on, Hearts supporters now looked forward to 3 May 2006 – for they knew that victory over Aberdeen at Tynecastle would secure a place for their club in the qualifying stages of next season's UEFA Champions League. Was history about to be made?

This is how the SPL table stood on 30 April 2006:

30 APRIL 2006

	P	W	D	L	F	A	Pts
Celtic	36	27	6	3	89	35	87
Hearts	36	21	8	7	70	29	71
Rangers	36	19	10	7	63	36	67
Hibernian	36	17	5	14	59	51	56
Aberdeen	36	13	14	9	44	37	53

MAY

And so the final chapter of this incredible season arrives and the month of May began as so many others had done in the preceding ten months – in controversy. After Hearts' demolition of the champions, Celtic's Neil Lennon accused Rudi Skacel of spitting at him during the game. The Czech Republic star vehemently denied doing this and his Hearts teammates and coach Valdas Ivanauskas backed him up. An impressive victory was somewhat overshadowed by the unsavoury aftermath of this incident. *The Sun* newspaper published a photograph of Skacel appearing to spit at Lennon. But the photo was far from conclusive and Skacel continued to furiously deny the accusation. And one wondered why *The Sun* waited until two days after the game to publish the photograph – were devious forces at work? Hearts certainly seemed to think so – the club banned the newspaper from Tynecastle with immediate effect.

3 May is a date synonymous with despair for all Hearts fans, given the events of *that* day in Dundee in

1986, but the date also means joy for this forty-something Jambo as it is the day my first grandson was born. Jack Peacock celebrated his first birthday on 3 May 2006 and his proud grandfather celebrated with him – before scurrying off to Tynecastle for the potentially historic fixture with Aberdeen. Hearts were now just three points away from a Champions League place. Tynecastle, as the cliché goes, was buzzing:

Hearts: *Gordon, Neilson, Pressley, Tall, Fyssas, Cesnauskis, Hartley, Aguiar, Skacel, Bednar and Jankauskas*

Given the roller-coaster nature of this astonishing season and the size of the squad now at Tynecastle, Hearts supporters were treated to an unusual sight as captain Steven Pressley led the team on to the park to an ecstatic welcome – for the Maroons were unchanged from Sunday's victory over Celtic. But the occasion was much too tense for a repeat of the free-flowing football that had torn the champions apart three days earlier.

Hearts were eager – perhaps too eager – to get an early goal to calm the frayed nerves of players and fans alike. Paul Hartley showed he was keen to take up from where he left off at the weekend when he delivered a sublime pass to Bednar. The Czech Republic striker laid the ball off for Cesnauskis but Chesny didn't connect properly and an early chance to put everyone at ease was gone – a pity because Aberdeen weren't at Tynecastle to enjoy the party. Following Hibernian's defeat by Rangers at Easter Road twenty-four hours earlier – a result which meant

Hearts still had business to attend to – the Dons clung to the hope that they had a chance of finishing in fourth place in the SPL which, if Rangers were to steal second place, would mean a UEFA-Cup place for Jimmy Calderwood's side. Aberdeen seemed to sense the unease among those of the maroon persuasion.

A mistake by Robbie Neilson almost let Foster through and he and Jamie Smith were causing problems for the normally rock-solid Hearts back four, particularly Takis Fyssas who looked uncomfortable all evening. Aberdeen's Steve Lovell had found his scoring touch of late so it wasn't the worst news in the world for the home team when the former Dundee striker had to leave the field injured after just half an hour. But his replacement was a player who has caused Hearts problems in the past – Darren Mackie.

Unsurprisingly, there was little creative football on display although Rudi Skacel fired in an effort from outside the penalty box that went close. As half-time approached and the game remained goalless, the apprehension in the air was palpable – Hearts knew that anything other than victory would leave an unwanted scenario of having to face Rangers at Ibrox on the last day of the season and having to avoid defeat to clinch second place – and none of us wanted that. Our apprehension turned to panic right on half-time when Richie Byrne had a free header at goal from an Aberdeen corner but his effort ended in the Gorgie Stand, much to the relief of the home fans.

Goalless at half-time, the occasion even appeared to affect the contestants of Hearts' Hit the Bar competition

– all fifteen of them failed to strike the crossbar and therefore win the top prize. It looked like becoming one of those nights.

Valdas Ivanauskas managed to get his message across during the break as Hearts started the second half on the offensive with Skacel and Cesnauskis driving forward at the Aberdeen defence. With the clock ticking away, however, we still anxiously awaited any real threat on goal. But, nine minutes into the second half, eureka! A corner kick from Skacel was flicked on by Eddie Jankauskas for Roman Bednar to apply the finishing touch. But Dons defender Russell Anderson punched the ball away from the Czech striker and referee Stuart Dougal immediately pointed to the penalty spot. That the referee only booked the Aberdeen player instead of sending him off is something only the official can explain. A fair proportion of the 15,000 Hearts fans turned their backs on the action at this stage, unable to look – even though it was the penalty expert Paul Hartley who was about to step up to the ball. But the Scotland maestro duly buried the penalty to give Hearts a precious lead and Tynecastle became an emotional cauldron.

There were still thirty-five minutes remaining and these would prove to be the longest thirty-five minutes of the season. Deividas Cesnauskis sprinted down the wing before delivering a brilliant cross that should have been converted by Bednar or Eddie J. but wasn't. Mikoliunas then replaced Rudi Skacel as Hearts seemed to be caught between going for a second, perhaps decisive, goal and shutting up shop.

Jankauskas then produced a fine piece of skill for

his countryman Cesnauskis but Chesny's effort went wide as the Hearts fans chewed on what remained of their fingernails. Mikoliunas then had an effort that went wide while, every time Aberdeen broke forward, the more pessimistic Jambos feared the worst. Then, with just ten minutes remaining, former Jambo Scott Severin lunged in with a two-footed 'tackle' on Bruno Aguiar and was shown a straight red card. Sevvy was a lifelong Hearts supporter as well has having played for his boyhood heroes for several years before his move north. If this was his way of helping his former employers to reach the Champions League, then it was very much appreciated by the home support who nevertheless chanted 'You used to play for a big team' as the midfield player trooped up the tunnel for an early bath.

Three minutes' injury time was played. Three long, emotionally draining minutes. With Tynecastle in a frenzy, Stuart Dougal eventually blew for the end of the match. Hearts had won 1–0. Hearts had secured second place in the SPL, thereby splitting the Old Firm. And, crucially, Hearts had earned a place in the qualifying rounds for the following season's Champions League.

The atmosphere inside Tynecastle at the end of the game was the most emotional I can recall in over thirty-seven years of following this damn team – even more emotional than the night Hearts defeated Bayern Munich in the quarter-finals of the UEFA Cup in 1989. An ecstatic Vladimir Romanov joined the players on the park for a lap of honour as the jubilant home support acclaimed their heroes. Forty-six years had passed since Hearts last played in the European Cup. Now they were back, albeit as runners-up in the SPL but the Champions League these days is composed of more than just the champions of European nations.

Ironically, the win over Aberdeen – the last Scottish team outside the Old Firm to play in the European Cup – came exactly twenty years to the day that Hearts infamously lost the league title at Dens Park in 1986. That day, Hearts fans wept as we ended in second place in the league. It was a sign of how much big money has influenced football when, two decades on, Hearts celebrated second place in the league as if they had won the league itself. But the runners-up prize in 2006 meant Hearts had a ticket to dine at Europe's top table. Two qualifying rounds would have to be overcome but the possibility of Heart of Midlothian taking on the likes of Real Madrid, Barcelona, Juventus, Manchester United and the rest was a prize worth celebrating in style!

The final game of this momentous league season was at Ibrox. Setanta Television would have been praying for Aberdeen to take something from Tynecastle in order to have a last-game showdown in Glasgow with the two clubs competing for Champions League football. But Hearts' triumph over the Dons meant the Ibrox encounter was little more than a chance for some of Hearts fringe players to show what they could do.

Hearts: *Banks, Barasa, Petras, Berra, Wallace, Beslija, Aguiar, Brellier, Skacel, Pospisil and Elliot*

Now, before you think I've become tired at the end of a long, hard season and have made up the Hearts team list, let me tell you that Valdas Ivanauskas had indicated after the victory over Aberdeen that he would rest some players for the trip to Ibrox – and he was as good as his word. Nine changes were made to the team that clinched Champions League qualification against the Dons, with only Rudi Skacel and Bruno Aguiar keeping their places. It was interesting to see Julien Brellier return to the team as it was believed by the Tynecastle hierarchy that Brellier and Aguiar were incompatible and couldn't play together. It's safe to say, however, that the Hearts team that took to the field at a half empty Ibrox (the official attendance was 49,792 – I'm assuming that was based on tickets sold, not just those fans who actually bothered to turn up) would not be the same one which would run out at Hampden six days later for the Scottish Cup Final.

The game against Rangers was largely a non-event, which few Hearts fans were complaining about, given the events of a quite astonishing season. Nearly one thousand of them made the trip to Govan and it was their antics that were the highlight of what quite frankly was a dull afternoon. Some Hearts wags unfurled a banner that declared they were at 'Ibrox Stadium – Champions League Section' and the travelling Jambos generally took the mickey out of their Glasgow hosts for most of the afternoon. An early indication of this came soon after the game kicked off when many of the travelling fans took out the Sunday papers and began reading them, the inference being that the game itself was of little interest to them.

Much changed Hearts may have been but they almost took the lead after just thirty seconds when Rudi Skacel – made captain for the day in the absence of Steven Pressley,

Paul Hartley etc. etc. – drove in a cross which skimmed across the Rangers six-yard area but, sadly, there were no takers to give Hearts a remarkably early lead. Hearts Reserves, with Beslija looking impressive, were playing some good passing football in the early stages although they had to thank Martin Petras for throwing his body in front of a Marvin Andrews effort to keep the scoreline blank. The ever-dangerous Kris Boyd then looked to finish off a move started by Lovenkrands but young Christophe Berra cleared the danger.

Mickey Pospisil then had a header saved by the Rangers keeper Wattereus but the action was very much half-hearted from both teams – a fact perfectly illustrated when Rangers' Kris Boyd found himself onside and all alone just eight yards from the Hearts goal. But the former Kilmarnock striker managed to hook the ball away from Craig Gordon's stand-in for the day, Steve Banks, and towards the safety of the less-than impressed Rangers support in the stand. It was an undoubted let-off for Hearts but Boyd had the last laugh ten minutes before the interval when he was given a free header at a Rangers corner to nod the ball past Banks and into the corner of the net. Although Bruno Aguiar was marking the back post, the Portuguese player thought it best to contribute to Rangers manager Alex McLeish's wellbeing by simply moving out of the way to let Rangers take the lead, which they held until the long-awaited half-time whistle blew.

The appearance during the interval of newly crowned world snooker champion Graham Dott – an avid Rangers fan by all accounts – was greeted by the Hearts support with the chant of 'There's only one Stephen Hendry'!

Hearts began the second half in brisk fashion and Skacel had the chance to score his first goal for several weeks when he latched on to a Pospisil pass, turned in the Rangers penalty box and fired in an effort that Wattereus did well to block. Julien Brellier then looked none too pleased to be substituted when Lee Johnson took his place. The Englishman made an early impression when he set up Aguiar with a fine pass. Bruno's effort was parried by the Rangers keeper and the ball fell to Pospisil. Unfortunately Mickey, in keeping with the general malaise, dragged his effort wide and the best chance to equalise was lost. With sixteen minutes left Rangers duly wrapped up the points when Kris Boyd slotted home Gavin Rae's pinpoint cross and the game duly ended.

It was Alex McLeish's last game in charge of Rangers and the home support gave him a generous if not totally rousing send-off. Several of the Hearts players who didn't take part in the game made it on to the pitch at the end to thank the Hearts fans who had gone to the effort to travel through to Ibrox. We all sincerely hoped that six days later those same players would be doing a lap of honour around Hampden Park with the Scottish Cup. A memorable league campaign was now over – the final day of an incredible season would take place at the national stadium on 13 May. Second Division Gretna stood between Hearts and a second Scottish Cup triumph in eight years. The build up to the occasion began almost before the fans arrived back from Ibrox.

The is how the final SPL table looked at the end of the season on 7 May 2006:

7 MAY 2006

	P	W	D	L	F	A	Pts
Celtic	38	28	7	3	93	37	91
Hearts	**38**	**22**	**8**	**8**	**71**	**31**	**74**
Rangers	38	21	10	7	67	37	73
Hibernian	38	17	5	16	61	56	56
Kilmarnock	38	15	10	13	63	64	55

WHEN THE HEARTS WENT UP TO LIFT THE SCOTTISH CUP . . .

In 1998, the last time Hearts won the Scottish Cup, the build-up was intense. Eight years later, I didn't sense the same intensity as Hearts prepared for their Hampden showdown. Perhaps this was due in part to the fact that Hearts' opponents were Second Division champions Gretna, who had just completed their own incredible season – just four years after gaining entry to the Scottish League, they were in their very first Scottish Cup Final. Perhaps it was because, having clinched the historic achievement of Champions League qualification, Hearts felt they had already attained their goal for this season. As Hearts had only won one major trophy in the last forty years, many might find this somewhat muted sense of anticipation to be a strange attitude but, as Hearts and Gretna took to the field at the National Stadium on 13 May 2006, I wasn't the only one among 35,000 Hearts fans in the crowd of over 51,000 who felt rather uneasy about the overwhelming-favourites tag that had been attached to the Maroons.

Hearts: *Gordon, Neilson, Pressley, Tall, Fyssas,*
Cesnauskis, Hartley, Aguiar, Skacel,
Jankauskas and Bednar

The Hearts team was back along familiar lines after the reserves had completed the league campaign at Ibrox six days earlier. The atmosphere at Hampden was simply brilliant as the Maroon Army filled three-quarters of the stadium with flag-waving, scarf-twirling bravado that brought a lump to the throat. But Hearts fans of old still knew the task ahead would be enormous. Gretna may have been lower-league opposition but their manager Rowan Alexander, with the help of ebullient owner Brooks Mileson, had built what was, in effect, almost a Premier League team: Alan Main was a goalkeeper of considerable ability and had played for St Johnstone and Dundee United; Steve Tosh had only recently left Aberdeen; striker James Grady counted both Dundee sides among his former clubs; while John O'Neil and Derek Townsley had quickly learned that, if you want to fulfil your dream of playing in a cup final, it's wise to leave Hibernian FC.

Gretna wanted to demonstrate they weren't overawed by the occasion and Grady set off towards Hearts goal straight from the kick-off. But Ibrahim Tall was alert to the danger and Hearts soon settled down and dominated the early stages. Paul Hartley fed Bednar but the ball just eluded the Czech striker. Then the Maroons almost secured the early breakthrough that would have soothed any lingering nerves when Deividas Cesnauskis picked up a deflected effort by Takis Fyssas and fired in a shot from just inside the penalty box. The ball smacked off the post as the eyes of the 12,000 Gretna fans behind Alan Main's goal momentarily closed.

It was encouraging for the maroon hordes to see Rudi Skacel eager to impress but a teasing cross from the Czech midfielder lacked the power to reach Jankauskas. Big Eddie then had a chance himself with an effort that Main did well to block but those Hearts fans who had placed large sums of cash on a thumping Hearts win were getting concerned that, after half an hour's play, there was still no score – particularly when Paul Hartley's threatening run on the Gretna goal fizzled out as he uncharacteristically overran the ball.

But it was far from one-way traffic towards the Gretna goal. Robbie Neilson came to the rescue when he cleared Kenny Deuchar's dangerous cross for a corner kick before, for the umpteenth time this season, Craig Gordon produced a brilliant save from Gavin Skelton's free kick to prevent the rank outsiders from taking a sensational lead. Skacel then set off on a run but, after making great progress to the Gretna penalty box, the midfield man was tackled as he tried to complete the job himself when the better option would have been passing to a clearly irritated Jankauskas.

Rather alarmingly, in the eyes of the Hearts support, it was end-to-end stuff – just what cup finals against lower-league opposition aren't meant to be. This was illustrated once again when the ever-dangerous Skelton fired in an effort that was a bit too close to Craig Gordon's goal for comfort.

Six minutes before half time, a goal finally arrived and,

much to the delight and relief of the Gorgie Boys, it came from the Maroons. Eddie J. nodded on a trademark Robbie Neilson throw-in for Rudi Skacel to drive the ball past Main and into the net from six yards out. Hearts fans leapt to their feet and we were able to breathe a little more easily during the half-time break.

If we thought Rudi's goal might have deflated our Second Division opponents, we were to be disappointed as the second half began. A superb move from Grady foxed Steven Pressley and gave Tosh the opportunity to equalise but the former Dons player drove his effort wide. We then looked to Paul Hartley as Hearts were awarded a free kick just outside the Gretna penalty box but the mid-field star's attempt at goal was too high. Aguiar had a go with a long-range effort that was never going to seriously trouble a goalkeeper of Alan Main's ability. And, next, Roman Bednar had a chance but his shot on goal soared high over the bar – an attempt that was more appropriate for Murrayfield than Hampden – and the Hearts fans' unease began to grow.

It intensified when Gretna should have equalised mid-way through the second half. Substitute David Graham was through on goal and rounded Craig Gordon. 35,000 Hearts fans may well have covered their eyes at this point, unwilling to witness Graham slotting the ball into the empty net. But, just as it seemed impossible for Graham not to score, Robbie Neilson made a tackle comparable to England's Bobby Moore against Brazil in the 1970 World Cup to save the day for Hearts and earn rapturous applause from those in maroon.

We looked for the second goal that would surely seal

the game for Hearts and a goal duly arrived – horrendously for the Jambos, it came as a result of a penalty for Gretna. Bednar pushed Grady inside the penalty box and, although Craig Gordon heroically saved Ryan McGuffie's spot kick, the Gretna player slotted the rebound home and headed off to dance in celebration with his teammates and their disbelieving supporters.

Pospisil and Brellier replaced Bednar and Aguiar respectively and Paul Hartley almost regained Hearts' lead with a shot from ten yards out which skimmed the crossbar. But, worryingly, it was Gretna who looked the likelier side to score with McGuffie and Chris Innes coming close. Referee Dougie McDonald blew his whistle for the end of ninety minutes with the teams tied at 1–1. Extra time beckoned and the looks of embarrassment on the faces of Hearts players and supporters alike told their own story.

The first real chance of extra time came when Skacel latched on to a pass from Pospisil but Rudi's effort struck the post and our agonies continued. Another Hartley free kick then took the tag of close but no cigar as players from both sides felt the effects of cramp. As a penalty shoot-out loomed, there were just five minutes to go when Skacel found himself through one-on-one with keeper Main. Rudi rounded the keeper but appeared to be tripped as he did so. The Czech stumbled but remained on his feet as we looked to referee McDonald to award the penalty. No foul decreed the official – a decision that incensed the Hearts players and support, most notably Paul Hartley who was booked for his trouble. An action Hartley regretted moments later when, having taken a kick from former Hibee Derek Townsley, promptly retaliated with a kick of his own. Referee McDonald showed Hartley a second yellow card followed by a red and furious Hearts fans greeted the end of extra time and the subsequent penalty shoot-out with anguish.

Pressley and Neilson scored the first two penalties for Hearts and Grady and Mark Birch did likewise for Gretna. Skacel then put Hearts ahead before the Hearts fans danced for joy as Craig Gordon saved Townsley's kick. So, after Mickey Pospisil netted Hearts' fourth penalty, Gavin Skelton knew he had to score to save the game. His shot hit the crossbar and Hearts had therefore won the Scottish Cup for the seventh time in their history.

It was bedlam at Hampden as the Hearts players and supporters danced for joy. There may well have been a tear in captain Steven Pressley's eye as he lifted the famous old trophy to tumultuous acclaim from the celebrating Hearts supporters.

There may also have been a tear in Brooks Mileson's eye at the end when he graciously took his players towards the Hearts support to applaud their contribution to a fabulous day. The Hearts fans cheerfully reciprocated by giving Gretna a standing ovation. It was a touching moment that – fittingly in the city of Glasgow – emphasised what football should be all about.

The scenes in Edinburgh that weekend matched those of 1998 as thousands of Hearts fans took to the streets of the capital the day after the win to welcome their triumphant side home. The Scottish Cup was proudly displayed as an open-top bus travelled along Princes Street, Haymarket, Dalry and Gorgie Road and back to